THE BEST
WINES
IN THE
S UPER
MARKETS
2021

NED HALLEY

foulsham
LONDON • NEW YORK • TORONTO • SYDNEY

W. Foulsham & Co. Ltd
for Foulsham Publishing Ltd
The Old Barrel Store, Drayman's Lane, Marlow, Bucks SL7 2FF

Foulsham books can be found in all good bookshops and direct from
www.foulsham.com

ISBN: 978-0-572-04805-1

Text copyright © 2020 Ned Halley
Series, format and layout design © 2020 Foulsham Publishing

Cover photographs © Thinkstock

A CIP record for this book is available from the British Library

Contents

——Why do we do it?——

Consolation. It's fair enough. In a year like this one, who wouldn't reach for a glass of wine? If you like wine, that is. Just a matter of choosing which one.

Welcome to *The Best Wines in the Supermarkets 2021*. It's an annual guide, and this is the seventeenth consecutive edition. It's an untypical one, because to date I have had the luxury of tasting most of the wines at events kindly laid on by the supermarkets. Every spring, they invite 'critics' like me to come along to interesting venues, invariably in London, to try the new vintages and new wines they will be offering in the year ahead.

It's brilliant. You get to taste genuinely representative cross-sections of each retailer's range. As many as 100, even 200, of the wines of which the buyers are most proud are opened for inspection. All you have to do is get invited and turn up.

Not so in 2020. In this year, only one of the big spring tastings actually went ahead. It was Aldi's event, held in splendour in London's Tate Modern art gallery early in March. I made it. Then bang. All the other events, most of them scheduled in May (Aldi likes to keep ahead) were cancelled as lockdown began.

Quick conference with the publisher of this book. I boldly asserted I'd be able to produce a timely and useful edition notwithstanding. Publisher acquiesced. Brave decision.

I started contacting the supermarkets for information. Absolute blank. Head offices appeared to have shut down, or at least to have gone into purdah, or furlough as we must now call it. Communications departments ceased communicating. But of course, as we all know very well, the supermarkets were extremely busy, on the front line, throughout lockdown. Never busier.

So I began joining the queues. Bought wines I was fairly confident would be worth reporting on. Tried them at home, made the usual notes. It was expensive and a lot of wine went down the sink until I found socially acceptable means of redistributing it. Over about four months of queuing, shopping, sniffing, slurping and scribbling I came up with the words.

The premise of the book differs from previous editions in several ways. One is that the wines were my choice rather than the supermarkets' choice. I organised my own tastings. Another is that I tasted the wines at home at comparative leisure instead of all in a row over a few hours amid a crowd of other writers. Another is that I paid for the wines. I felt their value – or lack of it – far more keenly than before. This is a consumer guide. And this year it's written very much from a consumer's point of view.

I hope my sense of personal commitment (and occasional grievance) comes across in the reports. My overall impression is that while the breadth of choice continues to narrow on supermarket wine shelves, as it has for years through austerity, Brexit angst and the advance of mass-market brands, there is still variety if you know where to look for it. There is impressively consistent quality too, and continuing value in spite of all the exigencies of taxation, currency fluctuation and climate change: heatwaves, droughts and fires (very serious ones in Australia and California in 2020) as well as the usual catastrophic floods, frosts and infestations to which European vine growers have long been resigned.

Vegan wines

Many wines sold in supermarkets are described as vegan. Real wine, after all, should consist solely of grape juice fermented by yeasts. That's it. Nothing carnal.

But wines are 'fined' (clarified and purified) using a variety of products. Some, including albumen, casein and gelatin, are animal-based. But alternatives such as bentonite clay and activated charcoal are reckoned just as effective.

As far as I can tell, wines labelled 'suitable for vegans' or similar are those fined with these mineral products. But it does depend what is meant by vegan. Some followers forbid food or drink produced with any animal involvement whatsoever. In winemaking this could proscribe grapes from vineyards fertilised with animal manure, or grazed by livestock. The world's grandest red wine, Domaine de la Romanée Conti, could be excluded: weeds between the famed Burgundian vines are controlled by horse-drawn hoe.

Value is a major factor in this book. If you buy wine in a supermarket, you are predisposed to seeking a bargain. My scoring system is rooted in value. The only wines that get included are those I believe are worth the money.

But there is growing pressure on price. This year, according to drinks industry figures, the average price paid for a bottle of still wine in the off-trade (that's in shops as distinct from bars etc) will rise above £6 for the first time. The prediction was made before the March 2020 Budget, when new Chancellor Rishi Sunak announced, unexpectedly, that he was freezing excise duty on all alcoholic drinks. Good news? Certainly, but it suggests that the Government was actually impressed by the representations of the industry. There have been duty freezes on beer, cider and spirits before, but this was the first freeze on wine duty for a very long time.

Perhaps Mr Sunak was heeding the words of my old friend Joe Fattorini, the distinguished (but larky) wine merchant, writer and broadcaster. 'It's time for a fairer deal for the 33 million wine drinkers in the UK', he told the trade press in the run-up to the Budget. 'Too many people still think wine is enjoyed by "wealthy" or "posh" people meaning price rises aren't a problem, but that clearly isn't the case. If the average price for a bottle of wine tips over the £6 mark as is predicted, we risk freezing out millions of hard-working people from a drink that they enjoy. The new Government has an opportunity to cut wine duty for the first time in over 35 years and give those people a break. I think it's high time they did so.'

Well, they didn't cut wine duty, but they didn't put it up either. And maybe, just maybe, the £6 frontier won't be crossed just yet. But don't hold your breath. It is possible that on 1 January 2021, when the UK's Brexit transition period expires, tariffs will be applied to imports from the EU. On still wine, that could work out at 7.5 pence per 75cl bottle and 20p on sparkling wine.

If you're reading this for the first time in 2021 and the UK Government has backed down, apologies for the anachronism. Otherwise, spare a thought for all the enterprises that will be saddled with the cost and administrative burdens of these new tariffs. As Miles Beale of the Wine & Spirit Trade Association put it in the midst of the lockdown during the summer, the new tariff regime 'will not increase choice for consumers, but instead will add an unnecessary barrier to trade. It is yet another blow to wine importers, independent wine merchants, pubs, and restaurants at a time when so many are already worried about their businesses and making finances go further'. Mr Beale added 'The shutdown of the hospitality sector has been hugely disruptive and this just adds to a long list of worries. Government needs to start listening to – and acting upon – suggestions from UK businesses, including taking action now to remove burden and costs on UK businesses and allow them to be more competitive to aid the UK's economic recovery.'

Amen to that. I like the idea of wine as a business as well as a pleasure having an important role in what will undoubtedly be a very long process of recuperation from the horrible effects of Covid-19 and its incalculable economic complications.

We all deserve some consolation, and I hope this guide will help you along the path to it.

Where does the best
——wine come from?——

It's France, I suppose. Fabled estates in Bordeaux, Burgundy and Champagne have a perpetual monopoly on the most-venerated red, white and sparkling wines, worldwide. If your budget per bottle starts at £100 I guess that's all you need to know. But for those of us who buy wine in supermarkets and consider even £10 a bit of a punt, the question needs to be readdressed.

In the global context, you could argue that the country of origin of any wine is immaterial. But the supermarkets wouldn't agree with you. They arrange all the wines in their stores and on their websites precisely according to their nationality.

It's quite odd. You wouldn't display your canned fruits and vegetables this way, would you? Or your frozen fish? Or anything else, really? But that's the way they do the wine and, accordingly, that's the way I arrange the listings in this book.

To be fair, the wines of particular nations and regions do have identifiable attributes even when made from a common grape variety. The white wines from fashionable Sauvignon Blanc, for example, have distinct styles at home in France's Loire Valley and away in the Marlborough region of New Zealand. Chilean Sauvignon has its own qualities, and so does South African.

Germany, though never in fashion, makes inimitably delicious wines from the Riesling grape. Australian wines from this noble variety are so different that I suspect uninitiated devotees of the Mosel and Rhine would hardly recognise a Clare Valley Riesling at all.

While the grape does much to determine the nature of the wine, location still counts for a lot. Landscape and soil conditions, weather and the peculiar skills and customs of the winemakers all have their parts to play.

The French have a word for it: *terroir*, which loosely translates as 'soil', but *vignerons* in France take it to mean the entirety of conditions local to the site of crop production. That's not just the soil but the lie of the land, its geographical position, its climate and indeed what the tillers of that soil and the custodians of the crops get up to.

On visits to France, I have heard much of terroir. Amid the most-valued vineyards of Chablis I have learned that the ground is composed largely of oyster shells, mountainised over millennia into vertiginous slopes. From these bleak, frost-ravaged heights come some of the world's most minerally luscious dry white wines. I've had it all endlessly explained to me and never really understood, but be in no doubt: *grand cru* Chablis is like no other wine.

And so on across all of France. Elsewhere, winemakers might not speak of terroir, but they all believe in the real or imagined unique properties of their estates. They all consider their wines to be an expression of their locations and traditions. This is what gives wine its much-treasured diversity, and of course its mystique. Wine is more than a mere nutritious drug. It's part natural phenomenon, part art form. Hurrah to that, I say.

It's all about the
grape variety

The grape, naturally, counts for everything in wine. The finished product is, after all, simply the fermented juice of the fruit. Well, yes, there will be a cultured yeast introduced to assist the process. And there are permitted additives, mostly sulphur products and clarifying agents, to ensure healthy, bright wine. The wine's natural sugars and acids can be supplemented.

But the grape variety still sets the pace. Dark-skinned grapes make red wine because the skins are included in the must (pressed juice) during fermentation and give the wine its colour. The juice of virtually all grapes is clear. You can make white wine with dark-skinned grapes by extracting the juice promptly and fermenting it free of the skins. The base wine for Champagne is made largely from dark-skinned grapes. But still white wine is made much more simply – from pale-skinned grapes fermented without their skins.

Different grape varieties produce correspondingly different wines. There are hundreds of distinct varieties, but a couple of dozen account for most production. All of us have favourites, or at least preferences. The varieties described here account for most of the wines on offer in the supermarkets.

Red wine varieties

Aglianico: Ancient variety of southern Italy said to have been imported by immigrant Greek farmers around 500 BC. The name is a recent rendering of former Ellenico ('Hellenic') and the grape has caught on again thanks to Aglianico del Vulture, a volcanic DOC of Basilicata. The wines are dark, intense, pungent and long-lived.

Barbera: The most widely planted dark-skinned grape of Piedmont in northwest Italy makes easy-drinking purple vigorous rasping red wine to enjoy young and also, increasingly, a darker, denser but still vigorous style given gravitas through oak-ageing. Mostly sold under denominations Barbera d'Asti and Barbera d'Alba. Unrelated to Barbaresco, a Piedmontese wine made from Nebbiolo grapes.

Cabernet Sauvignon: Originally of Bordeaux and the mainstay of claret, Cabernet berries are compact and thick-skinned, making wine of intense flavour and gripping tannin. The grandest wines need decades to develop their full bloom. Everyday wines made worldwide typically have dense colour, purple in youth, aromas of blackcurrants and cedar wood ('cigar box') and firm, juicy-savoury fruit.

Gamay: It's the grape of Beaujolais. Colour can be purple with a blue note; nose evokes new-squashed raspberries with perhaps a pear drop or two, the effect of carbonic maceration, the Beaujolais method of vinification. Fruit flavours are juicy, bouncing, even refreshing.

Grenache: The French name for the Garnacha, originally of Spain, where it is much employed in Rioja and other classic regions. HQ in France is the southern Rhône Valley with further widespread plantings across the country's Mediterranean regions. Wines can be light in colour but emphatic in flavour with a wild, hedgerow-fruit style lifted with spice and pepper. Widely cultivated across the New World.

Malbec: The signature grape of Argentina. A native of Bordeaux, where it plays a minor blending role, it thrives in the high-altitude vineyards of Mendoza, a province of the Andean foothills. The best wines have dark colour and a perfume sometimes fancifully said to evoke leather and liquorice; flavours embrace briary black fruits with suggestions of bitter chocolate, plum and spice.

Merlot: Bordeaux variety very often partnering Cabernet Sauvignon in claret blends and also solo in fabled Pomerol wines including Château Petrus. The grape is large and thin-skinned compared to Cabernet, making wine of rich ruby colour with scents evoking black cherry and cassis and fruit that can be round and rich. Ordinary wines are soft, mellow and early developing but might lack the firmness of tannin that gives balance.

Pinot Noir: It's the solo grape of red burgundy and one of three varieties in champagne. Everyday Pinot wines typically have a bright, translucent ruby colour and aromas evoking red soft summer fruits and cherries. Flavours correspond. Fine Pinot has elegant weight and shape, mysteriously alluring. New Zealand makes distinctive, delicious, sinewy Pinots; Chile produces robust and earthy Pinots; California's best Pinots compare for quality with fabulously expensive Burgundies.

Sangiovese: The grape of Chianti, so-named after the Latin for 'the blood of Jove', makes pleasingly weighted, attractively coloured wines with plummy perfume, even pruny in older wines, and slinky flavours evoking blackcurrant, raspberry and occasionally nectarine. Good Chianti always has a clear tannic edge, giving the wine its trademark nutskin-dry finish.

Syrah: At home in southern France, the Syrah makes wines that at their best are densely coloured, rich in aromas of sun-baked blackberries, silky in texture and plumply, darkly, spicily flavoured. The grandest pure-Syrah wines, such as Hermitage and Côte Rôtie, are gamey, ripe and rich and very long-lived. Syrah is widely planted across Mediterranean France as a blending grape in wines of the Côtes du Rhône and Languedoc. Under the name Shiraz, Syrah is Australia's most prolific red-wine variety.

Tempranillo: The grape at the heart of Rioja has to work hard. The unique selling point of the region's famous red wines is the long ageing process in oak casks that gives the finished product its creamy, vanilla richness – which can all too easily overwhelm the juiciness and freshness of the wine. The Tempranillo's bold blackcurranty-minty aromas and flavours stand up well to the test, and the grape's thick skin imparts handsome ruby colour that doesn't fade as well as firm tannins that keep the wine in shape even after many years in cask or bottle. Tempranillo is widely planted throughout Spain, and in Portugal, under numerous assumed names.

White wine varieties

Albariño: Rightly revered Iberian variety once better known in its Minho Valley, Portugal, manifestation as Alvarinho, a mainstay of vinho verde wine. Since the 1980s, Albariño from Spain's Galicia region, immediately north of Portugal, has been making aromatic and scintillatingly racy sea-fresh dry white wines from vineyards often planted close to the Atlantic shore. The seaside DO of Rias Baixas, now a major centre for gastro-tourism, is the heart of Albariño country. The variety, characterized by small, thick-skinned berries with many pips, is now also cultivated in California, New Zealand and beyond.

Chardonnay: Universal variety still at its best at home in Burgundy for simple appley fresh dry wines all the way up to lavish new-oak-fermented deluxe appellations such as Meursault and Montrachet making ripe, complex, creamy-nutty and long-developing styles. Imitated in Australia and elsewhere with mixed success.

Chenin Blanc: Loire Valley variety cultivated for dry, sweet and sparkling white wines, some of them among France's finest. Honeyed aromas and zesty acidity equally characterize wines including elegant, mineral AOP Vouvray and opulent, golden late-harvested

AOP Coteaux du Layon. In South Africa, Chenin Blanc now makes many fascinating and affordable wines.

Fiano: Revived southern Italian variety makes dry but nuanced wines of good colour with aromas of orchard fruit, almonds and candied apricots and finely balanced fresh flavours. Fleetingly fashionable and worth seeking out.

Glera: Widely planted in the Veneto region of northeast Italy, it's the principal variety in prosecco sparkling wine. The grape itself used to be named prosecco, after the winemaking village of Prosecco near Treviso, but under a 2009 change to the wine-denomination rules, the name can now be applied exclusively to the wine, not the grape. Glera makes a neutral base wine with plenty of acidity. It is a prolific variety, and needs to be. Sales of prosecco in Britain have now surpassed those of champagne.

Palomino Fino: The grape that makes sherry. The vines prosper in the *albariza*, the sandy, sun-bleached soil of Andalucia's Jerez region, providing a pale, bone-dry base wine ideally suited to the sherry process. All proper sherry of every hue is white wine from Palomino Fino. The region's other grape, the Pedro Ximenez, is used as a sweetening agent and to make esoteric sweet wines.

Pinot Grigio: At home in northeast Italy, it makes dry white wines of pale colour and frequently pale flavour too. The mass-market wines' popularity might owe much to their natural low acidity. The better wines are aromatic, fleetingly smoky and satisfyingly weighty in the manner of Pinot Gris made in the French province of Alsace. New Zealand Pinot Gris or Pinot Grigio follows the Alsace style.

Riesling: Native to Germany, it makes unique wines pale in colour with sharp-apple aromas and racy, sleek fruit whether dry or sweet according to labyrinthine local winemaking protocols. Top-quality Rhine and Mosel Rieslings age wonderfully, taking on golden hues and a fascinating 'petrolly' resonance. Antipodean Rieslings have more colour and weight often with a mineral, limey twang.

Sauvignon Blanc: Currently fashionable thanks to New Zealand's inspired adoption of the variety for assertive, peapod-nettle-seagrass styles. Indigenous Sauvignons from France's Loire Valley have rapidly caught up, making searingly fresh wines at all levels from generic Touraine up to high-fallutin' Sancerre. Delicate, elegant Bordeaux Sauvignon is currently on top form too.

Semillon: Along with Sauvignon Blanc, a key component of white Bordeaux, including late-harvested, golden sweet wines such as Sauternes. Even in dry wines, colour ranges up to rich yellow, aromas evoke tropical fruits and honeysuckle, exotic flavours lifted by citrus presence. Top Australian Semillons rank among the world's best.

Viognier: Formerly fashionable but perpetually interesting variety of the Rhône Valley makes white wines of pleasing colour with typical apricot aroma and almondy-orchardy fruit; styles from quite dry to fruitily plump.

More about these varieties and many others in 'A wine vocabulary' starting on page 158.

——Brand awareness——

Big-brand wines such as Blossom Hill and Hardy do not crowd the pages of this book. I do get to taste them, and leave most of them out. I believe they don't measure up for quality, interest or value.

The best wines in the supermarkets are very often own-brands. Own-brands date back to the 1970s, when interest in wine finally began to take root in Britain. Sainsbury's was first, with its own Claret, about 1975. It was hardly a revolutionary idea. Grand merchants like Berry Bros & Rudd (est 1698) had been doing own-label Bordeaux and much else besides, for ever.

In the supermarket sector, wine was bought on the wholesale market like anything else, from butter to washing powder. Only when interest in wine started to extend beyond the coterie served by the merchants did the mass retailers take any notice. It was thanks, of course, to the new craze for foreign travel, and to the good influence of writers like Elizabeth David, who revealed the joys of Continental-style food and drink. In 1966, Hugh Johnson's brilliant and accessible book *Wine* piqued the public consciousness as never before.

The adoption of supermarket wine was slow enough, but accelerated in the 1980s by the arrival of new, decent wines from Australia. Earlier on, cheap Aussie wines had been overripe, stewed rubbish, but breakthrough technology now enabled fresh, bold reds and whites of a different stripe. Wretched Europlonk brands like Hirondelle retreated before a tide of lush Chardonnay and 'upfront' Shiraz.

The horizon for supermarket wine buyers, always shackled by price constraint, was suddenly widened. In spite of the delivery distances, southern hemisphere producers could match their Old World counterparts for value as well as interest and quality.

In time, the winemakers of Europe fought back. Top estates carried on with 'fine wine' production, but humbler enterprises had to learn how to master real quality at the everyday level. They did. I believe the huge improvements in the simpler wines of the Continent owe much to the need to match the competition from the New World.

By the 1990s, Britain had become the world's biggest wine importer. Supermarkets were largely responsible, and now had muscle in the market. They started to dispatch their own people to vineyards and wineries worldwide, not just to buy the wines but to participate in their production. And always, they demanded the lowest-possible prices.

And so to today's proliferation of supermarket own-brands. They are the flagships of every one of the big grocers, and usually the focal point of promotions. They are, naturally enough, the wines of which their begetters are most proud. Mass-market brands do still persist in the supermarkets. Some are very good. I think of Blason, Chasse and Vieille Ferme from France; Baron de Ley and Miguel Torres from Spain; McGuigan and Penfolds from Australia; Catena from Argentina and Concha y Toro from Chile, among others.

If you have a favourite popular brand, do check the index to this book on page 187. It might not be mentioned in the entry for the supermarket where you're used to finding it, but that doesn't mean I've left it out.

Pick of the year

Of the 27 top-scoring wines this year, France accounts for 12. Even though it's been a most unusual year for tasting wine, as well as in many other respects, this is very much the average French performance. Of course it's subjective, but I was asked in a press interview recently to name my desert island country when it comes to wine (it's the sort of question interviewers inevitably ask) and I found myself replying Italy. It was an instinctive answer, and certainly the honest one. At home, we prefer Italian wine.

Well, no surprise that Italy comes second for top scores this year, though way behind France, with 5. Spain next with 4, Germany and Portugal next on 2 apiece. Chile and England complete the set with 1 each. Nothing for Australia or South Africa this year.

Does it signify? It's true that 'New World' wines have steadily been losing UK market share to European-producing nations in recent years, but not to the point of extinction. Big-selling 'global brands' like Barefoot, Gallo, Hardy's and so on do of course all hail from the New World, but none of these has ever (or will ever, I venture) appear here. But great individual wines are of course made on the more-distant continents, so I'm sure we can look forward to future triumphs from further afield.

In the chart of retailers, again no surprise. Waitrose comes top for top scores with 6. Well yes, just 6. Tesco is right behind with 5, followed by the Co-op with 4. Aldi, M&S and Sainsbury's tie on 3 apiece, Morrisons gets 2 and Asda 1. For what it's worth, I believe that's quite a fair reflection.

Red wines

Castellore Puglia Primitivo 2018	Aldi	£4.99
Raoul Clerget Beaujolais 2019	Morrisons	£5.00
Cuvée Chasseur 2019	Waitrose	£5.49
Tesco Douro 2017	Tesco	£6.00
Molise Biferno Riserva 2016	Co-op	£8.00
Ventoux Paul Jaboulet Aîné 2018	Tesco	£8.00
M Chapoutier Côtes du Rhône Villages 2018	Tesco	£9.00
El Duque del Miralta Rioja Crianza 2015	M&S	£9.50
Les Nivières Saumur 2017	Waitrose	£9.99
Terre de Faiano Primitivo 2019	Waitrose	£9.99
The Cubist Garnacha 2017	Waitrose	£9.99
Waitrose Douro Reserva 2017	Waitrose	£11.49
M&S Classics No. 36 Bourgogne Pinot Noir 2018	M&S	£12.00

White wines

Exquisite Collection Leyda Sauvigon Blanc 2019	Aldi	£5.49
Dr L Riesling 2018	Asda	£7.00
Vanita Grillo 2019	Co-op	£7.00
Taste the Difference Greco di Tufo 2018	Sainsbury's	£8.50
M&S Classics No. 2 Mineralstein Riesling 2019	M&S	£9.50
Marques des Los Rios Rioja Blanca Reserva 2016	Morrisons	£13.00
Taste the Difference Pouilly Fumé 2019	Sainsbury's	£13.00

Sparkling wines

Balfour Foxwood 1503 Cuvee	Co-op	£17.00
Les Pionniers Champagne Brut	Co-op	£19.00
Champagne Philizot Brut 2012	Aldi	£19.99
Finest Premier Cru Champagne Brut	Tesco	£20.00
Sainsbury's Blanc de Noirs Champagne Brut	Sainsbury's	£21.00
Finest Grand Cru Blanc de Blanc Champagne Brut 2012	Tesco	£26.00

Fortified wine

Waitrose Blueprint Amontillado
    Sherry   Waitrose   £7.69

Aldi

Aldi was the easy one. The ever-expanding discounter managed to hold its big 2020 wine tasting before the March lockdown. Sadly it was the only supermarket chain that did. Plenty of good wines here, although I found most of the under-£5 reds a lot less impressive than their prices. I suppose we no longer have any right to expect decent wine at under a fiver, when the excise duty and VAT take up the first £3.30 of a £5 bottle and £3.05 of a four-pounder. That sub-£5 wines exist at all is wonder enough, given the minimum-price regulations (at least 50p per unit of alcohol) already in force in Scotland and Wales, and likely soon to extend UK-wide.

There is nevertheless a formidable choice in Aldi at around a fiver. While I have left out the disappointments, I have high-scored one Chilean red at £4.99 and top-scored a Puglian also at £4.99. I've found six decent rosés, the only expensive one the £9.99 English wine, included out of patriotic fervour. Otherwise, all but a couple of the still wines are under £7.

I very much liked the Chilean white wines, ranging from £3.99 to £5.49 – the latter a Leyda Sauvignon Blanc I scored 10. And there are good sparklers, from an unexpected Alsace crémant at £8.29 to a fabulous vintage champagne, Philizot 2012 at £19.99 – another top score.

Not every wine (including that champagne) is available in store. Aldi has rapidly developed its online offering and this has no doubt been kept very busy during the viral crisis. It's a good clear website so don't despair of getting hold of the online-only wines I've noted as such.

RED WINES

8 Buenas Vides Bonarda 2019 £4.99

Summer barbecue red, I've noted, rather dismissively perhaps. It's a briary, gently spicy, confection of decent heft from the elusive Bonarda grape originally of Italy's Piedmont and you do get some of the region's bounce in the juicy flavour; 13.5% alcohol.

9 Exquisite Collection Uco Valley
Malbec 2019 £5.99

Smart package delivering a darkly plump and satisfyingly complete variation on the theme with trademark roasty ripeness and spice; not exactly a nuanced wine, but honest and good value; 13.5% alcohol.

8 Exquisite Collection Organic
Mendoza Malbec 2019 £6.99

I liked this just as much as the preceding Uco Valley wine but it's £1 more, perhaps to cover the additional impost of organic cultivation and vinification. It's plummy, spicy and full with 13.5% alcohol.

8 Exquisite Collection South Australia
Shiraz 2018 £5.79

A curiously pale colour for Shiraz but there's masses of bright, sweetly-baked, ripe (14.5% alcohol) black fruit here with convincing weight and balance; a roast pork wine.

9 Estevez Chilean Carignan 2019 £4.99

Carignan grapes are usually left unidentified in hearty Mediterranean blends but here it gets star billing from Chile's Central Valley in a dark, roasty, steak-and-chips red with plenty of guts and grip; 12.5% alcohol.

RED WINES

FRANCE

🍷 8 **Pierre Jaurant Fitou Reserve 2018** £4.99
Spicily perfumed Languedoc middleweight with pleasing
blackberry roundness and a brisk edge of acidity; 12.5%
alcohol.

🍷 8 **Pierre Jaurant Cahors Malbec 2018** £5.49
The red wines of Cahors in the Midi's baking Lot Valley
have always been made from Malbec grapes (known
locally as the Cot) but now the variety has outpaced the
locality in celebrity – thanks to Argentine Malbec. This
is a subtler wine than the Mendoza kind but pleasingly
spicy and grippy in its dark, black-fruit charm; 13.5%
alcohol.

🍷 10 **Castellore Puglia Primitivo 2018** £4.99
If you like the plump chocolate style of southern Italian
Primitivo you'll really like this: it's juicy and complex as
well as darkly dense and savoury with good heft and best
of all a trim balancing acidity; 13% alcohol. Remarkable
at this price.

ITALY

🍷 8 **Castellore Italian Aglianico** £4.99
A pale lightweight non-vintage pasta red from the sun-
swept hills of Campania with a likeably gripping baked-
fruit savour; 12.5% alcohol.

🍷 8 **Specially Selected Valpolicella
Ripasso 2017** £7.99
Every supermarket now does a Ripasso (see glossary) and
here's a competitively-priced contender with recognisable
pruny fruit, appreciable weight and a firmly puckering
finish. 13.5% alcohol.

RED WINES

9 Animus Red 2017 £4.99

Unidentified grape blend, but an identikit Portuguese red with dark, clovey and minty briar fruit. It has good heft (13% alcohol) and a reassuring sleekness. In spite of the gimmicky package I'm rather taken in.

8 Cambalala Pinotage 2019 £4.99

The distinctive treacly-savoury style in this moderately hefty (14.5% alcohol) indigenous Cape wine should suit winter stews (or curries) and burnt offerings from the summer barbecue alike.

8 Grapevine Cabernet Sauvignon £3.79

Purple-coloured, juicy, youthful (though non-vintage) blackcurranty middleweight from the great plain (and wine lake) of La Mancha; a balanced and wholesome party wine of real worth; 12.5% alcohol.

**8 Baron Amarillo 80-Year-Old
Vine Red 2016** £6.99

The antiquity mentioned in the name is that of the vines rather than the wine – and 80 is a better age for a vine than for a wine like this, so that's all good then. The grapes are mainly Bobal, a thick-skinned variety widely planted around Valencia (whence cometh this wine) to add colour and acidity to the region's robust red. This one is softly ripe with cassis and vanilla dominant but trim and balanced; 13% alcohol.

RED WINES

USA

🍷 8 **The Wrangler Big Chief Blend 2016** £6.99

Surprise Californian blend including Cabernet Sauvignon, Pinot Noir, Syrah and several more seemingly random components which nevertheless make for a cohesively enjoyable, earthily ripe, plump and juicy all-round red for just about any occasion; 14% alcohol.

PINK WINES

CHILE

🍷 8 **Estevez Colchagua Rosé 2019** £5.99

Brightly presented Merlot-based party-frock pink has plenty of raspberry–strawberry fruit in a convincingly fresh framework, finishing winningly fresh; 12.5% alcohol.

ENGLAND

🍷 8 **Specially Selected Lyme Bay English Rosé 2019** £9.99

All credit to Aldi for listing this Devonshire contrivance. Mostly from Pinot Noir grapes, it's pale salmon-pink in colour, has an encouraging cherry whiff and keen matching fruit, 12% alcohol. It's outrageously expensive for what it is, but the cause is noble.

FRANCE

🍷 8 **Maison Sur Littoral Rosé 2019** £5.99

It comes in a blue bottle so you don't get to see the delicate shell-pink hue until you've got it home, but it's a decent Mediterranean wine, crisp and tangy with red-berry notes; 12.5% alcohol.

🍷 8 **Pierre Jaurant Languedoc Rosé 2019** £5.99

Pale and quite interesting dry seaside pink; delicately bright with red summer fruit complete with a citrus lift; 12.5% alcohol.

PINK WINES

 8 Specially Selected Costières de Nîmes Rosé 2019 £6.49
This proper food wine has bold smoked-salmon colour, eager red-fruit aroma and crunchy dry berry flavours in nifty balance; a grown-up rosé from a dependable appellation of the warm south; 13% alcohol.

 7 Rozetta Pink Chardonnay 2019 £4.99
Yes, Chardonnay makes only white wine but there's a drop of Dornfelder here too to turn the colour a pale onion hue; otherwise it's a conventional appley-floral dry chardy with a bit of residual sugar and modestly priced; 12.5% alcohol.

WHITE WINES

 8 Exquisite Collection Padthaway Chardonnay 2018 £5.99
Steady wholesome balanced everyday wine from evocatively named but remote Limestone Coast region south of Adelaide, capital of South Australia, so-named in honour of Queen Adelaide, consort of our own King William IV. I always think Aussie chardies taste more interesting if they can be imbued with a sense of place; 13.5% alcohol.

 8 Kooliburra Australian Semillon 2019 £5.99
Exotic colour and perfume from this interesting aperitif or salad-matching just-dry wine evoking sweet pineapple and peach ripeness; 14% alcohol.

WHITE WINES

AUSTRALIA

🍷 **7** **Exquisite Collection Clare Valley**
Riesling 2018 £6.99
This racy-limey hallmark Clare Riesling has been much praised over time, but this is the same vintage I tasted last year, so it can't have sold all that well and it's lost some freshness; if you find the 2019, do try it; 11.5% alcohol.

🍷 **9** **Estevez Chilean Chardonnay 2019** £3.99
Generous in colour, apple-blossom-evoking whiff and sweet-but-crisp corresponding fruit; a very proper Chardonnay, lively, fresh and long, at a very keen price; 13% alcohol.

🍷 **10** **Exquisite Collection Leyda Sauvignon**
Blanc 2019 £5.49
Artful rival to very much costlier Loire appellations has intriguing asparagus/peapod aromas, lush-mineral grassiness and long, generously ripened classic Sauvignon flavours; 13% alcohol. A brilliant construct at this price, from a region of Chile first planted with vineyards less than 30 years ago.

CHILE

🍷 **9** **Estevez Chilean Viognier 2019** £5.49
The colour is positively yellow, and the fullness of ripe exotic fruits – apricot to the fore – is matchingly intense; a lush but dry aperitif wine (or with grand shellfish?) that tastes way above price; 13.5% alcohol.

🍷 **8** **Exquisite Collection Touraine Sauvignon**
Blanc 2018 £5.99
Zesty Loire very-dry moules wine – grassy, lemony and convincing; 12.5% alcohol.

FRANCE

WHITE WINES

FRANCE

♆ 8 **Pierre Jaurant Picpoul de Pinet 2019** £5.99
Understandably popular Mediterranean party dry white;
has a briny twang with a discreet residual richness in the
fruit; 12.5% alcohol.

♆ 8 **Pierre Jaurant Roussanne Pays
d'Oc 2019** £5.99
Peachy Mediterranean dry white brimming with tropical
fruit-salad flavours and balancing out well; 14% alcohol.

ITALY

♆ 9 **Castellore Italian Pecorino 2019** £4.99
From the coastal vineyards of Pescara in the Abruzzo, a
grassy-fresh, near-austere dry wine with a crafty lushness
happily typical of the new-wave dry whites of Italy. I
can't fault it, especially at this price; 12.5% alcohol.

♆ 8 **Forza Della Natura Unfiltered
Catarratto 2019** £4.99
Sicilian 'Force of Nature' wine, please note, has not
been submitted to the unnatural rigours of clarification
and might just have a faint haze, but the flavours are
crisply lively and multi-faceted; jolly interesting and more
sensibly priced than your typical 'natural' wine; 12%
alcohol.

♆ 8 **Castellore Italian Fiano 2019** £5.49
I fear ancient-world variety Fiano's recent revival might
be fading, but here's a Sicilian version that nicely conveys
the orchard-fruit, hint of nectar, lifting citrus note
formula; 13% alcohol.

WHITE WINES

NEW ZEALAND

🍷 9 **Freeman's Bay Pinot Gris 2019**   £5.99
Made firmly in the Alsace style, extracted, smoky and pungent – a million miles from the vapid Pinot Grigio (same grape) of the Veneto – and an attention-grabbing, stimulating off-dry aperitif; 13% alcohol.

🍷 8 **Specially Selected New Zealand
        Grüner Veltliner**   £6.49
This gently spicy spin on Austria's indigenous GV is pretty dry in style but has the right prickly fruit and freshness to make it a versatile food match – fish, fowl and any kind of Asian flavour; 13% alcohol. If it has a dated vintage, I didn't note it.

PORTUGAL

🍷 8 **Cerqueira Alvarinho 2019**   £6.49
It's from Portugal's Minho Valley, home to vinho verde, but this is another kind of wine: well-coloured, tangy-fresh and long of lush, saline white-fruit flavours, bright and stimulating; 12% alcohol.

SOUTH AFRICA

🍷 8 **Specially Selected Cambalala Chenin
        Blanc 2019**   £5.99
Crisp but with a creamy-honey note in the right Chenin Blanc tradition this might be a bit austere for some tastes but scores for refreshment value; 12.5% alcohol.

SPAIN

🍷 8 **Baron Amarillo Rioja Blanco 2018**   £4.49
New-style dry white Rioja (how I always hope for an antiquated oaky old version) has a lick of richness from the Viura grape and a little lemon lift; 13% alcohol.

SPARKLING WINES

9 **Exquisite Collection Crémant d'Alsace** £8.29
The 'creaming' sparkly wines of Alsace are underrated and undersupplied in Britain and more or less extinct in supermarkets, so full marks (well, 9 out of 10) to Aldi for listing this rarity with its creamy mousse, exotic fruit and brut-dry freshness; 12.5% alcohol. It's 'seasonal' so more likely to be on sale around Christmas. Stock up.

8 **Veuve Monsigny Champagne Brut** £12.49
This safe bet has a lemony twang to the fruit but is by no means green and has a crafty richness at the edge of the fruit; 12% alcohol.

8 **Veuve Monsigny Rosé Champagne Brut** £16.99
Boldly coloured, strawberry scented and brightly fresh pink fizz; the genuine article; 12.5% alcohol. Online only.

10 **Philizot Champagne Brut 2012** £19.99
A mature champagne from a legendary vintage that is really quite special, mellow in colour as well as in bakery aromas and creamy-streamy fruit briskly balanced with citrus notes; it's not cheap champagne, it's serious champagne, and a true bargain; 12.5% alcohol. Last year, they were selling the underwhelming 2014 vintage and this is a vast improvement. Sadly available only online.

8 **Valdobbiadene Prosecco Superior** £7.49
If you must drink prosecco, this is at least well made and sensibly priced. It's quite dry in style with hallmark elderflower character; 11% alcohol.

FRANCE

ITALY

Asda

I enjoyed my visits to the two Asda stores nearest my home in Somerset, and found 25 or so wines to write about. The ranges on shelf seemed diminished from previous outings, but I may be imagining it. What I do know is that by 2019, when the proposed merger with Sainsbury's collapsed, Asda management had already reduced their wine range drastically. I fear that process has continued.

This year one of the highlights is Dr L Riesling, a scintillating German bargain (£7) that until last year was always on sale in Sainsbury's. How odd that it should pop up in Asda instead in 2020.

Elsewhere in the range, there seems a growing proportion of brands like Barefoot, Gallo and McGuigan and a thinning out of the once-marvellous Extra Special own-label wines. My top picks this year do include Extra Special Yarra Valley Pinot Noir from Australia and, get this, Extra Special English Sparkling Brut – from Surrey.

So why did I particularly enjoy my visits to the Asda stores? I can only say that despite the bizarre obligations of social distancing, both were populated by the friendliest and most helpful staff and, dare I mention it, the most friendly and obliging customers too. I am particularly grateful to the gentleman who helped me find my car amid the labyrinthine windings of the car park.

There's something benevolent about Asda. I know the business is up for sale and the future is uncertain, but I hope it continues to prosper.

RED WINES

ARGENTINA

♟ 8 **Extra Special Malbec 2019** £7.50
Wholesomely roasty black-fruit winter red balances sweet
savour and grippy spice; 13.5% alcohol. I paid just £6 in
a 'rollover' promo.

AUSTRALIA

♟ 8 **Extra Special Barossa Shiraz 2018** £7.00
Great big (14.5% alcohol) cushiony Shiraz in the
traditional Aussie style but not overripe; it's grippy with
savoury black fruits and obliging tannins; a safe bet at a
realistic price.

♟ 9 **Extra Special Yarra Valley Pinot
Noir 2018** £9.00
Delicate cherry colour and the transcending smell of
raspberries ripe under a hot Australian sun mark this
elegant wine by distinguished De Bortoli as something
particularly special. The fruit is silky and lively with
summer red berry fruits, finishing trim and bright; 13%
alcohol. If the 2019 arrives, do try it.

CHILE

♟ 8 **Extra Special Carmenère 2018** £6.50
The Carmenère grape, now widely adopted in Chile,
supposedly gets its name from the carmine-coloured wine
it makes. It's certainly one of the attractions of this one
from Colchagua, rich in fruit as well as hue, with cassis
perfume and black-cherry and chocolate-plum notes;
13.5% alcohol. A great accompaniment to a summer
barbecue or a winter stew.

RED WINES

FRANCE

🍷 8 **Costières de Nîmes Cuvée Réserve 2018** £7.00
Dependable brand for the singular peppery style of this appealing southern Rhône appellation; intense in brambly fruit, sun-roasted but juicy and lifted; 14% alcohol.

ITALY

🍷 8 **Extra Special Barbera d'Asti 2018** £6.50
Nice rendering of the bouncy brambly Barbera of Piedmont, a well-coloured juicy wine made likeably silky by oak contact; 13% alcohol.

🍷 9 **Burdizzo Chianti Riserva 2015** £7.00
Slinky oak-framed proper cherry-raspberry fruit of healthy weight and balance in this very decent riserva – an aged style of Chianti usually rather expensive and not always inspiring. I liked this a lot, especially at this price; 12.5% alcohol.

🍷 8 **Villa Vincini Gran Rosso 2018** £8.00
An unexpected blend of Merlot (of Bordeaux fame) and Corvina, the grape of Valpolicella, this makes a deep purple, cherry and blackberry melange of easy, juicy charm with a notable clean finish to the ripe flavours; 14% alcohol. The 2019 should compare well.

PORTUGAL

🍷 8 **Extra Special Douro 2018** £6.50
Stark graphic label and a low price attracted me to this out-of-the-usual Douro, and it's really not bad: warm porty nose and convincingly dense blackcurrant fruit hinting at mint, spice and liquorice; 13.5% alcohol.

RED WINES

PORTUGAL

🍷 8 **Bodacious Vinho 2017** £8.00

A proper oddity by enterprising Portuguese winery Falua, this bullish Alentejo blend unites Cabernet Sauvignon with local grapes Aragonez and Castelão to make a hearty, plummy dark food red with textbook Portuguese notes of clove and cinnamon; 13.5% alcohol. I think it's great; if the 2017 has been superseded by 2018 or even 2019, do try it.

SPAIN

🍷 8 **Extra Special Marques del Norte
Reserva Rioja 2015** £8.50

Dense colour just showing a little orange with ageing; the vivid blackcurrant fruit is at ease with the vanilla from oak contact; it's still grippy with tannin and should go on for years; 14% alcohol.

PINK WINES

FRANCE

🍷 8 **Le Cellier de Saint Louis Provence
Rosé 2018** £8.50

Impressive Varois pink with a delicate pale coppery colour, fresh fruit-tree and floral aromas and crisp red-fruit flavours, very dry-finishing with clear citrus and 13% alcohol. I found it on 'rollback' offer at £7 – a bargain well worth looking out for.

🍷 8 **Luminière Rosé 2019** £9.00

I found this Provence pink on 'rollback' too (see wine above) at £7.50 and after liking it last time round, was pleased with the attractive shell-pink colour, elegant poised dry cool pink flavours and twang of citrus; 13% alcohol.

Asda

PINK WINES

ITALY

🍷 8 **Diverso Negroamaro Rosé 2019** £7.00
Lots of magenta colour in this bold Puglian pink, matched
by assertive not-quite-dry red soft summer fruit flavours;
12% alcohol.

WHITE WINES

AUSTRALIA

🍷 8 **Extra Special Barossa Valley
Chardonnay 2019** £8.00
Part of the blend is fermented, reportedly, in oak casks
and you can just about get the sweet-nut (coconut?)
richness imparted to the authentic Barossa sweet-apple-
ripe style; it's absolutely dry, 13.5% alcohol and sensibly
priced.

FRANCE

🍷 9 **Languedoc AOP Blanc 2019** £7.00
Determinedly anonymous blend of Grenache Blanc,
Marsanne and Bourboulenc constructs a very pleasing
fruit salad of orchard and stone fruit flavours successfully
trimmed up with correct citrus acidity; 12.5% alcohol.
Good price for this quality, and I got mine at £6 on
'rollback'.

🍷 8 **Limoux 2018** £9.50
Chardonnay of real character from a Pyrennean outpost
better known for sparkling Blanquette wine, this is
warmly sweet-apple ripe with long, slaking fresh flavours;
13% alcohol. Mystifyingly, the price has been hiked
mountain-high from last year's £7.00

WHITE WINES

GERMANY

🍷 **10** **Dr L Riesling 2018**   £7.00
Inspiring fresh, racy and affordable moselle from the incomparable Dr Ernie Loosen, leading light of German winemaking. In its distinctive elegant blue bottle (mosel wines are supposed to come in green), it delivers the coolest, purest minerality of lush, ripe green apple flavour; 8.5% alcohol. A happy discovery at Asda. I am still cross with Sainsbury's for delisting it two years ago. If you find the 2019 vintage, pounce.

🍷 **8** **Extra Special Soave Classico 2019**   £6.25
Verona's picturesque white lives up to the, er, suaveness of its name in this agreeably blanched-almond-rich yet lemony-fresh manifestation; 12.5% alcohol.

🍷 **8** **Diverso Falanghina 2018**   £7.50
From Beneventano in the Campania region of southwest Italy, a zingy aperitif dry wine with notes of greengage and grapefruit in the aroma and the addition of pear and even pineapple in the flavour; fresh, fanciful stuff and fun; 12.5% alcohol

ITALY

🍷 **8** **Lugana 2019**   £9.50
From the shores of Lake Garda comes one of northeast Italy's lesser-known wines, so all credit to Asda for persisting with it, albeit up in price by £1 from last year. Orchard-fruit flavour, succulently ripe with nectarine notes, balanced by an almost spiky citrus acidity. A real attention-grabber; 13% alcohol.

WHITE WINES

Asda (side margin)

NEW ZEALAND

🍷 **8** **Extra Special Sauvignon Blanc 2019** £7.50
Lively Marlborough wine with ripe gooseberry aromas, lots of grassy-green fresh tangy fruit and reassuring suggestions of asparagus; 12.5% alcohol.

PORTUGAL

🍷 **8** **Bodacious Branco 2019** £8.00
Companion to the cheery Bodacious red (see under Asda reds) from the Alentejo region near Lisbon a concentrated stone-fruit and floral dry wine with character and balance; 12.5% alcohol.

ROMANIA

🍷 **9** **Wine Atlas Feteasca Regala 2018** £5.25
Much-praised softly lush peach'n'pineapple not-quite dry wine with artful crispness and lemon tang; 11.5% alcohol. I haven't tasted the 2019 but at the price, it would hardly constitute a risk to give it a try. One of the few remaining lines in Asda's Wine Atlas range, I do like the food-matching suggestion: hard cheese and turkey. What?

SPAIN

🍷 **9** **Extra Special Rueda Verdejo 2019** £6.00
This hits the spot. From the emerging Rueda region of Castille it's crisply bright with tangy white fruit and a distinct lemony lift, very dry but plenty of interest and 13% alcohol. Party-wine price but summer-food-matching quality.

WHITE WINES

🍷 **8   Viña Sol 2019**   **£7.50**
You can buy Viña Sol, Spain's best global-brand dry white,
made by the marvellous Torres company in Catalonia,
just about everywhere but I'm placing it in Asda because
in 2020 I found it on 'rollback' offer at £5.50. Now that
is a proper bargain for this racy, green-but-ripe, satisfying
refresher; 11.5% alcohol.

🍷 **8   Extra Special Albariño 2019**   **£9.00**
Big flavours of seaside freshness combining apple
crispness and peach ripeness in artful balance, a strong
match for shellfish or exotic Asian flavours; 13%
alcohol.

SPARKLING WINES

🍷 **9   Extra Special English Sparkling Brut**   **£21.00**
Made by Denbies in Surrey from a blend of Chardonnay
(grown in Hampshire, I gather), Pinot Meunier and
Pinot Noir – the champagne formula – this is a serious
attempt to replicate the French model. And it succeeds,
proving the brioche aroma, creamy orchard fruitiness and
luxuriant mousse can all be transferred to Blighty. This is
a single-vintage wine – all the fruit is from the glorious
2015 harvest – and is ageing with the same grace you'd
expect from a decent champagne; 12% alcohol.

FRANCE

Asda

SPARKLING WINES

8 **Extra Special Crémant de Loire Brut** £9.00
Nicely balanced dry sparkler from Chenin Blanc that
shows off the grape's capacity for combining ripeness of
fruit with zinginess of fresh acidity; a fine 'creaming' wine
very much in its own style; 12% alcohol.

9 **Extra Special Champagne Premier
Cru Brut** £21.00
Much-improved house champagne by Louis Bernard
offers mellow bakery aroma and corresponding ripe
orchard-fruit flavours in a fine tiny-bubble mousse
capped by an easy citrus edge; 12.5% alcohol. Often
reduced to £19.

The Co-operative

The Co-op tasting is particularly important for me, because it's the one chance I get to try a real cross-section of the range. There are no Co-op outlets near me with more than a small selection of the wines, and the Co-op does not do an online wine service.

I have visited half a dozen branches in western England to accumulate the wines mentioned here, and I suppose I should be pleased I found as many as are featured on the following pages – just over 30 of them.

When it comes to finding the more interesting wines, do not overlook the Co-op's Wine Locator service. As revealed in this space last time, you go to the Co-op home page on your computer or mobile smartphone device, click on Co-op Food and then on Wines. There's a Find a Wine search box. Type in the name of the wine, go to the 'find this product' box, put your postcode in and you'll get a list of the nearest branches stocking it.

RED WINES

ARGENTINA

🍷 9 **Co-op Fairtrade Irresistible Malbec 2019**   £7.50
Affecting sweet-briar smell from this inky maroon pure Malbec promises all the intensity and savour of the grape made the Argentine way, and it delivers; smoothly juicy and long and all the better for coming from long-standing Fairtrade producer La Riojana at Famatima; 13% alcohol.

🍷 9 **Vinalba Finca La 70 Malbec Cabernet Sauvignon 2018**   £9.00
Another cracking vintage for this lavish Patagonian blend, in which I imagine the Cabernet contributing the slick cassis element in the briary-blueberry compote of flavours that makes this such a memorable wine, from the immediate aftertaste to the wistful recollections; 14% alcohol.

AUSTRALIA

🍷 9 **The Unexpected Red 2019**   £6.50
'A sensationally smooth and rich experience awaits the adventurous' says the Co-op in commending this pot-luck blend by Andrew Peace. It mixes Bordeaux grapes Cabernet Sauvignon and Merlot with Rioja variety Tempranillo and Italy's Sagrantino – and it works: dense maroon colour, clinging but short-of-jammy blackberry/blackcurrant fruit and brisk dry finish; 14% alcohol. Perhaps most unexpected of all is the price – it's genuinely cheap for what it is.

RED WINES

AUSTRALIA

🍷 8 **The Interlude Pinot Noir 2019** £6.85
Aussie Pinot often has more garnet in its colour than its raspberry-red Burgundian counterpart, and here's an example. You do get raspberries, with English cherries, in the aroma and fruit, and an all-round earthiness; drink it cool; 13% alcohol.

🍷 9 **Château Vieux Manoir 2019** £7.00
The new 2019 is as dependably ripe and claret-like as its lively but comfortingly rounded precursors. It's darkly ripe with a sweet-black-cherry savour framed by still-firm tannin, vivid and satisfying; 13.5% alcohol.

🍷 8 **Côtes du Rhône La Grange**
   St Martin 2017 £7.75
Dependable perennial: deep beetroot colour, muscular, spicy and complete in a decent vintage for the region; 13.5% alcohol. Not sure what the label description 'Reserve' means. Drink now.

FRANCE

🍷 8 **Domaine des Ormes Saumur 2018** £8.00
I loved the 2016 vintage of this Loire beauty, but cannot find the succeeding vintage (2018 is a guess) in any of my accessible branches but the Co-op is still listing it. I urge anyone with a suitable handy store to seek it out. Assuming, that is, you warm to the inimitable style of Loire red wine from Cabernet Franc grapes typified by my description of this wine last time: purple hue, bright blueberry aroma, crunchy-leafy juicy flavours and aboundingly ripe, even round, in its exhuberant fruit.

RED WINES

🍷 8 **Réserve de Pizay Beaujolais**
       Villages 2019   £8.00

This is a perfectly good everyday Beaujolais with the unusual added flourish of an estate name, and a nice drawing of a château on the label. On the back, you can read of the adventures of Co-op wine buyer Ben Cahill, whose job it is to 'galavant around the globe, find and slurp wines' (sic). That'll be 'gallivant', Ben. Attractive bright wine, quite full in fruit with pear-drop notes; 13% alcohol.

🍷 9 **Château Millegrand Cuvée Aurore**
       Minervois 2018   £10.00

I wonder if this new addition from the Languedoc to the list is to make up for the dropping of the gorgeous Pic-Saint-Loup Les Grandes Costes (top scorer here last year) in 2020. I'll miss the Pic, but this handsomely presented sleek and spicy Syrah-based monster (14% alcohol) is very consoling indeed. The Minervois AC, near Carcassonne and named after a Roman temple dedicated to Minerva, used to make little other than weedy rubbish but now has several serious producers, and this is one of them. Price is very fair.

🍷 9 **Château Beau Site 2014**   £22.00

Presumably selling slowly, this rather grand *cru bourgeois* St Estèphe claret can only be improving with time, and is the same price as last year, when I tasted it and much admired its opaque colour, luxurious perfume and savour; 13% alcohol. Lovely wine with years of development ahead.

RED WINES

ITALY

9 Vanita Negroamaro 2018 £7.00

This brilliant choc'n'cherry Puglian red is smooth and
savoury; ripe (14% alcohol) but not sweet, grippy and
even abrading; a great match for pasta. It's the counterpart
to the inspired Vanita Grillo (see Co-op whites) with a
similarly styled old-fashioned heraldic label. The horrible
plastic cork was the only nasty surprise.

8 Co-op Irresistible Barbera d'Asti
Superiore 2016 £7.50

Darkly juicy but nicely gripping black-cherry and bramble
pasta red with proper Barbera bounce and balance;
slinky, developed and impactful with 14.5% alcohol.

10 Molise Biferno Riserva 2016 £8.00

Utterly consistent Montepulciano-grape-based blend
from obscure DOC south of the Abruzzo in Italy's east
midlands is a revelation: sweetly ripe and perky in the
Montepulciano manner but with pruny-plummy facets
and a silkiness from ageing in cask that I find irresistible,
especially at the nugatory price of eight quid; 13%
alcohol. Last time I visited Giorgio Locatelli's lavish
restaurant in London (admittedly it was a while ago), this
very wine was the house red.

RED WINES

ITALY

🍷 **8** **Longobardi Cuvée Isabella Chianti 2018** £8.50
Generic wine from London-born John Matta, whose Castello Vicchiomaggio estate in Chianti Classico country supplies several lines at The Co-operative. This is sleek with firm cherry-raspberry fruit flavours and is brightly balanced in the proper Italian Chianti tradition; 12.5% alcohol.

🍷 **8** **Longobardi Collezione Paolo Chianti 2018** £8.75
The Co-op is clearly taken with the manifold productions of Mr Matta's Chianti estates. This one, new to me, is a yeoman screwtop wine of little pretension but lots of concentrated proper Chianti cherry-briar fruit tightly framed by tannin with a bit of oak-contact; 12.5% alcohol. Not cheap, but I got mine at £7.75 on promo and suspect it will continue to be reduced from time to time.

🍷 **9** **Casa Nardelli Cuvée Carolina 2018** £9.00
It would be Chianti but for this lovely Tuscan wine's inclusion of one part Cabernet Sauvignon to its nine of the DOCG-approved indigenous Sangiovese grape, which excludes it from classification as Chianti. The makers may have made the right decision, though, as this is a formula that works: silky, spicy and succulent in the best oak-aged Chianti style with a very correct lifting nutskin-dry finish; 13.5% alcohol.

RED WINES

PORTUGAL

🍷 9 **Vila Real Rabelo 2017** £6.00

From the Port country, the Douro Valley, a simple red from Touriga Nacional grapes, the main constituent of the great fortified wines for which the region is justly famous. This is a soft midweight with easy elderberry-plum-briar fruits and a clean edge; 13.5% alcohol. The strange helix-bodied cork, a rare sight indeed, is intended to be pulled out by hand.

SPAIN

🍷 8 **Corte Mayor Rioja Crianza 2016** £9.00

Ornately presented crianza wine which might seem pricey until you taste it and recognise that its statutory year in wood has been in new oak casks (very expensive), imparting creamy vanilla richness into the abundant juicy cassis fruit. Producer Baron de Ley describes it as a 'confident' wine and you can tell what is meant; 13.5% alcohol.

PINK WINES

FRANCE

🍷 9 **La Vieille Ferme Rosé 2019** £7.75

Charming bottle has chickens on the label – always a very good sign – and a clear view of the pleasing coral-coloured wine within. Made by Rhône royalty the Perrin family – who make the much celebrated Miraval Rosé for Brad Pitt and Angelina Jolie – it has hints of strawberry and redcurrant in the bouquet and flavours, coming over very fresh and stimulating; really very good indeed, for a rosé; 12.5% alcohol.

PINK WINES

8 Sensi Toscana Rosato 2019 £8.00

ITALY

It's from Chianti country and made with the resident red grape, the Sangiovese. Nice rose-petal colour and matching floral nose lead to a proper pink-tasting palette of flowery, herby flavours trimmed up with a nice twang of citrus; 12.5% alcohol.

WHITE WINES

9 Las Moras Pinot Grigio 2019 £7.00

ARGENTINA

This is a very different manifestation of the puzzlingly popular PG of northeast Italy. It's apple-crisp and tangy with grapefruit notes and yet palpably plump with blanched-almond creaminess; tastes expensive and satisfying; 12.5% alcohol.

9 Andrew Peace Chardonnay 2019 £5.50

Remarkably sunny and fresh Victoria State dry but exotically ripe bargain Chardonnay of the old school; 12.5% alcohol. Absolute snip at this price.

9 Laneway Chardonnay 2018 £8.50

AUSTRALIA

Expressionist-style label illustration is a bit of challenge but this Victoria wine is something of an old master: rich even 'buttery' in the way of the Aussie chardies of yesteryear, it's barrel-fermented which makes it peachy and luscious, but it's lifted into minerality and brightness by a tangy acidity; 14% alcohol. Clever stuff, great fun and good value.

WHITE WINES

AUSTRIA

🍷 9   **Eitzinger Grüner Veltliner 2018**   **£8.50**

Austria's flag-bearing grape the Grüner Veltliner is rightfully in vogue, and this is consistently among the best on the market. From the Kamptal, one of the most-favoured vineyard zones west of Vienna, this is richly coloured, gently spiky with white-pepper sprinkled apple and pear aromas, and exotic matching fruit flavours; 12.5% alcohol. Fine aperitif and an equally good match for fish or fowl.

🍷 8   **La Vieille Ferme Blanc 2019**   **£7.75**

This white counterpart to the fine rosé (see page 55) from chicken-admiring Rhône outfit Perrin is generous with peachy, pear and pineapple lushness with lifting citrus twang; 13% alcohol. A very dependable buy.

FRANCE

🍷 8   **Co-op Irresistible Marsanne 2019**   **£8.00**

Artful (I don't mean the label) dry white by Languedoc monster Jean-Claude Mas makes the most of the intriguing Marsanne grape: fresh aromas of apple flesh and crisp cabbage, peachy-melon fruits with a lick of creaminess, all with a citrus twist; 13% alcohol.

🍷 8   **Alsace Gewürztraminer**
      Wolfberger 2018   **£9.25**

Well-coloured wine with instantly recognisable lychee and rose Gewürz aromas and I agree with the Co-op that there is even a touch of Turkish Delight here; long smoky-spicy flavours, grapily ripe rather than sweet and a citrus twist; 12.5% alcohol.

WHITE WINES

 Château Roumieu Sauternes 2016
half bottle   £10.00
Ambrosial 'dessert' wine from a Sauternes estate
neighbouring the great Château Climens. A perfect balance
of succulent, honeyed richness and brisk, lime-tinged
freshness (13.5% alcohol); its flavours linger, they do not
cloy; gorgeous wine at a fraction of the price of the high-
status names from this appellation.

FRANCE

 Co-op Irresistible Chablis 2018   £12.50
The gold shot with green colour – a Chablis hallmark
and perhaps as much of the imagination as of the eye – is
a nice prelude to the flinty-luscious classic style of this
quintessential wine by renowned producer JM Brocard,
who has been supplying the Co-op since 2008. Special-
occasion wine, a heavenly match with any shellfish but
especially lobster, at a sane price for what it is; 12.5%
alcohol.

Shhh It's Riesling 2019   £6.00
Well I never. To me, the Co-op has always represented
the best traditions of Methodist primness in all its doings
(well, apart from the tragic venture into banking) and yet
here we are mired in scatology. Or perhaps the team in
Manchester didn't notice the dooble-entendre. The wine
is a straight, green-apple, crunchy fresh, one-dimensional
dry moselle, perfectly agreeable – and cheap; 11.5%
alcohol.

GERMANY

WHITE WINES

GERMANY

🍷 9 **Reichsgraf von Kesselstatt Riesling**
     Kabinett 2018   **£12.00**
The Co-op always lists a classic Riesling from the Mosel's extensive and admirable Kesselstatt estate, but never in large quantities (check online for your nearest stocking branch), and on a very random quality-style basis. Last year it was a magnificent Spätlese; this year it's a Kabinett. Look, I haven't tasted this one, but if you're a fan of great QmP wine, hurry out after this one, because it can be relied on to be magnificent, and a gift at £12; 9% alcohol.

ITALY

🍷 8 **Verdicchio dei Castelli di Jesi 2019**   **£6.00**
Delicate and inoffensively sweet green-fruit regional speciality wine from Ancona in Italy's dreamy Marches, an easy-drinking lunch-party dry white at a modest price; 12.5% alcohol. The amphora-shaped bottle and Botticelli Venus are a kitsch delight.

🍷 10 **Vanita Grillo 2019**   **£7.00**
I do like the ornately heraldic label on this outstanding Sicilian wine – its scrolly pretensions might just be a nod to the crumbling charms of the island's baroque architecture. The tangy nectarine-grapefruit freshness of the wine, counterpointing the tropical fruit at the centre of the flavour, equally manifest the joyous nature of Sicily's modern winemaking tradition – featuring grapes like the Grillo, once lost in the sticky labyrinth of marsala, now to the fore among the new ranks of scintillating Sicilian dry white wines; 12.5% alcohol.

WHITE WINES

NEW ZEALAND

🍷 **8** **The Ned Sauvignon Blanc 2019** £9.50
Now-ubiquitous brand brilliantly named after a peak in the Marlborough valley of Waihopai; nettly, grassy flavours, wildly refreshing. I paid £7.50 on promo; 13% alcohol.

FORTIFIED WINES

PORTUGAL

🍷 **9** **Sandeman Fine White Port** £10.00
The bottle comes in a wasp-yellow box bearing the bold image of The Don, Sandeman's enduring icon (since 1930) and the wine doesn't disappoint. It's amber rather than 'white' and certainly sweetly porty but with a correcting acidity that makes this such a fascinating aperitif wine. Drink it very well chilled, and you'll discover that Port does have its variations; 19.5% alcohol.

SPARKLING WINES

ENGLAND

🍷 **10** **Balfour 1503 Foxwood Cuvée** £17.00
A reprise of last year's wildly enthusiastic report, with one adjustment: the price has reduced by 50p to £17.00. It should be as tasted in 2019, but is so good it may well have mellowed with extra time in bottle. From Chardonnay and Pinot Noir planted in 2002 at the Hush Heath estate (est 1503) in Kent, this is a 'brut' style of fine-bubble sparkling wine of pale gold colour with farmhouse-loaf aroma and mellow ripe orchard fruit surging flavours; 11.5% alcohol. A Co-op exclusive that makes you proud to be British.

SPARKLING WINES

🍷 10 Les Pionniers Champagne Brut   £19.00

'We can't tell you who makes it', says the Co-op, 'but we can tell you you'll be hard-pressed to find a better fizz for less than twenty English pounds!' Well said, I say, and of course this champagne is made for the Co-op by Piper Heidsieck (est 1834), and named in honour of the Rochdale Pioneers who founded the first modern co-operative society in 1844. This Chardonnay-led wine has an alluring lemon-meringue-pie nose, ripe white fruits in a fine persistent mousse and abounding freshness; 12% alcohol.

FRANCE

Lidl

The 'core' range of about 80 wines at Lidl is by far the smallest offering from any of the retailers featured in this guide. Over the years I must have tasted all the wines, and have written about the modest number that seem interesting or good value.

I am always looking for improvements, and have been regularly assured by Lidl's wine team that the core range is set for expansion. But there's little to report right now.

Of course the principal attraction of Lidl's wine section is the Wine Tour. Six times a year, a new selection of a dozen or so, usually with a theme such as Mediterranean, New World or what-have-you, is introduced. And when they're gone, they're gone, as the Lidl slogan puts it with commendable candour. Which puts all the wines well beyond the scope of this book.

Given how good some of the Wine Tour selections have been, I can only hope Lidl might one day consider co-opting the pick of them for more consistent duty.

RED WINES

AUSTRALIA

8 Winemaker's Selection Coonawarra Cabernet Sauvignon 2018 £5.99

Proverbial upfront fruit in this pure Cabernet from Coonawarra, reckoned the grape's natural home in South Australia. It's big, juicy with blackcurrant intensity, and wholesome; 13.5% alcohol.

FRANCE

8 St Emilion Grand Cru 2016 £10.99

Very decent follow-up to the successful 2015 vintage of this wine, which kind of launched Lidl into the 'fine wine' firmament a few years back. This is dark and intense, already-developed recognisable St Emilion with sleekness and spice to the mellow black-cherry Merlot-led fruit; 14% alcohol. It could do with more time in bottle.

ITALY

8 Squinzano Riserva 2015 £5.99

Wonderfully named Puglian DOC (Squinzano is 'the twelfth most populous town in the province of Lecce') has warm, even baked, blackberry fruit and evocative plump ripeness of the simmering south, with the benefit of maturity; 13% alcohol. Not a core wine, but a regular seasonal one.

8 Barolo 2014 £11.99

I nipped into Lidl not long before deadline and found this 2014 vintage, as recommended in this space last year. It's £11.99 now instead of the £9.99 starting price so I didn't buy one, but I'd guess the time in bottle has done it no disservice. It's a good vintage (best so far for this core wine) with limpid coppery-ruby colour, whiff of cherries, roses and truffle, easy weight, quite silky, savoury and tight-finishing; 14% alcohol.

RED WINES

PORTUGAL

♍ 8 **Azinhaga de Ouro Douro Reserva 2017**   £5.99
Table wine from Port country; dark and spicy in the
tradition of the fortified version but middling in weight,
though not at the cost of intensity or interest; oak contact
provides creaminess to the texture; 13.5% alcohol.

SPAIN

♍ 8 **Baturrica Gran Reserva 2012**   £4.99
Long-aged though this formidable Tarragona is, you feel
it could comfortably cope with another restful decade
before truly rounding out. Meantime, it's a big, tough,
baked-fruit confection with pungent mulberry-briar fruit,
still grippy with tannin though modestly inflammatory
at a mere 13% alcohol; looks smart with its arty label
and gold-wire cage, and suits chilli dishes, as you might
expect.

♍ 8 **Cepa Lebrel Rioja Reserva 2014**   £5.49
This is an ordinary enough Rioja, middling in weight
but forthcoming with the sweet vanilla cassis fruit and
clean balance; 13.5% alcohol. I cannot think of another
Reserva on the market at anything approaching this
price, so it must have a mention.

WHITE WINES

CHILE

♍ 8 **Cimarosa Pedro Jimenez 2018**   £4.29
Wild lemon-melon aroma from this foothills-of-the-Andes
wine leads into a bracingly brisk and dry white with a
rather exotic set of spicy nuances. The Pedro Jimenez,
better known as Ximenes or PX at home in Andalucia
where it is the sweetening grape for dark, rich sherry, is
unrecognisable in this wild mountain wine, but might just
appeal if you like this sort of thing; 12% alcohol.

WHITE WINES

FRANCE

🍷 **8** Mâcon-Villages 2018 £6.99
This decent brassica/peach/trace-of-spearmint typical Mâconnais (Burgundy outpost) chardonnay is fresh and bright.
Safe buy from the core list even if the price is no particular
bargain; 12.5% alcohol.

ITALY

🍷 **8** Botte Conti Pecorino 2018 £5.25
From the Terre di Chieti in the Abruzzo, home of the
Pecorino grape, this dry and cheerfully zesty thoroughly
Italian refresher is lively and bright; 12% alcohol. It's
new to the core range and I'm sure the 2019 will follow.

NEW ZEALAND

🍷 **9** Cimarosa New Zealand Sauvignon
Blanc 2019 £5.99
Good first impression from the tangy crisp gooseberry
fruit on nose and palate from this Marlborough wine,
and the theme is followed through in terms of freshness
and lingering flavours; 12.5% alcohol. If I'm sounding
cautious it's because the price is uncommonly reasonable
for a Kiwi wine. I guess this is an uncommonly good buy.

SOUTH AFRICA

🍷 **8** Cimarosa South African Chenin
Blanc 2018 £3.99
I know it's very cheap but I prefer this to Lidl's
Winemaker's Selection South African Chenin Blanc at
£5.99. This one is a fresh, wholesome dry everyday wine
with an elderflower scent, meadow-sweet white fruit,
trademark honey trace of Chenin and a brisk, lemony lift
at the edge of the flavour; 12.5% alcohol.

WHITE WINES

SPAIN

🍷 8   **Abellio Albariño Rias Baixas 2018**   £5.99
Perennial Galician dry white, attractively labelled with an arboreal theme, delivers keen, briny flavours evoking the Atlantic breezes that air the Albariño grapes ripening on the high trellises traditional in the seaside vineyards; 12.5% alcohol.

🍷 8   **CEO Godello Monterrei 2019**   £7.99
It might have been a 'Wine Tour' item but this sticks in the mind and I must include it. The name, of course, was the draw – the perfect gift for the Chief Executive Officer in your life. This allure aside, it's a keen fresh example of in-vogue Godello from Galicia with a seaside tang and a relishable ripe orchard-fruit heft; 12.5% alcohol.

SPARKLING WINES

FRANCE

🍷 8   **Crémant de Loire Brut**   £8.49
Floral nose, creaming mousse and ripe white-fruit flavours make for a refreshing but also a nuanced sparkler of obvious quality; it's mostly Chenin Blanc and has fine balance, topped up with Chardonnay; 12% alcohol. A much better buy than Lidl's Comte de Senneval Champagne (too much sugar in the dosage, I believe).

Majestic

I haven't been to a Majestic tasting for two years and am out of touch. Following the bizarre separation of the business from its succubus-like subsidiary Naked Wines and subsequent sale to some Japanese bank, I really thought the whole thing would go to pot. Majestic featured in every edition of this guide up to 2019, but in 2020 I left it out. Not enough to say.

But there are developments. After much speculation about its future, including rumours all the branches would be renamed Naked Wines or be closed altogether in favour of an online-only operation, there were management changes and a new commercial boss called Robert Cooke took the helm.

'Majestic's historic strengths have always been around sourcing exciting, unusual wines, and having the expert store staff on hand to extoll their virtues', he told the trade press. It was the first sensible thing I'd heard from a Majestic manager in a long time. 'In recent years', Mr Cooke continued, 'it wouldn't be unreasonable to say we have lost that focus. So I tasked the teams with curating new ranges they would be proud to stock. Wines which excite our customers and our store staff in equal measures. We are focusing back on our heartlands, those interesting parcels at the lower-premium end, which producers love making and wine lovers love exploring. There's also a lot of brilliant wines lost to the range over recent years which we have now brought back in too.'

That's good enough for me. I've tried a few Majestic wines – including a handful of old favourites – for this mini entry, and hope to expand back into full coverage of the range next time round.

Majestic long-ago dumped the 12-bottle minimum purchase that so artfully launched the business as a 'warehouse' operation. These days you can buy just one bottle if you're so-minded. But Majestic don't want you to do that. Buy at least six bottles, and you'll qualify for the Mix Six discount. It applies to all the wines, but at differing percentages, so every one of them is tagged with paired prices, as shown for those featured in the following pages.

RED WINES

🍷 8 Château Guiot Costières de Nîmes 2017 £7.99/£9.99

A Majestic stalwart from the earliest days, this vigorous fruits-of-the-forest Languedoc Grenache-Syrah is on top form: grippy ripe (13.5% alcohol) dark fruits with the appellation's hallmark pepperiness and intensity. The 2018 vintage can't be far behind.

🍷 8 Côtes du Rhône Belleruche 2018 £9.99/£11.99

Biodynamic wine by Rhône legend Michel Chapoutier is intense in flavour rather than weight and spiffingly poised between juicy black silky fruitiness and peppery, grippy mouthfeel; 14.5% alcohol.

🍷 8 Santenay Vieilles Vignes Girardin Père et Fils 2016 £24.99/£28.99

Back in the day, burgundies from Vincent Girardin were a bit of a staple at Majestic. Now, the Girardin name is corporate owned but the wines are still good. This village red from a fine, maturing vintage is silky, earthy and brimming with creamy strawberry-raspberry fruit, light in style but beautifully shaped and finished; 13% alcohol.

FRANCE

🍷 9 Primo Appassimento 2018 £8.99/£9.99

Don't let the retro poster-art labelling deter you from this Puglia Primitivo-Negroamaro mix. The winemaker, says Majestic, "twists the stems of every grape bunch. It's laborious work but allows berries to fill with concentrated juice." Intense deep maroon colour and corresponding spicy black-fruit flavours edged with baked ripeness; 14.5% alcohol. Thank you very much to Paul and Lettie for putting me on to this wine.

ITALY

RED WINES

**8 De Forville Langhe
Nebbiolo 2018**   **£9.99/£11.99**

Majestic has been listing De Forville wines since time began, and there are still several on the go, including this vivid young cherry-bright but intensely savoury variety from the Barolo and Barbaresco grape at prices on a very different scale. This is clingy, even spirity, and a fine match for sticky pasta, probably best drunk now; 14% alcohol.

**9 Valpolicella Ripasso Classico
Superiore La Casetta 2017**   **£14.99/£16.99**

A marvellous revisit to this succulent, intense raspberry-juicy speciality wine from Verona. "Simply fabulous stuff" I wrote of the 2000 vintage (£9.99) in my 2005 book. Enticing as ever, weighty with ripe fruits, minty, poised and trimmed with the edge of bitter-sweet abrasion of amarone fruit; 14% alcohol.

PINK WINES

**8 Château de Pennautier
Rosé 2019**   **£9.99/£11.99**

Pennautier wines from Cabardès north of Carcassonne proliferate at Majestic. This alluring shell-pink, blossom-scented dry but firmly flavoured wine includes, unusually for the region, Merlot grapes along with the indigenous syrah and grenache, and does hold the attention; 13% alcohol.

WHITE WINES

FRANCE

8 Hunawihr Pinot Gris 2017 £9.99/£11.99
From an interesting range of Alsace wines at Majestic –
much more interesting than you'll find in any supermarket
– this is a simple fresh PG with attractive smoky pear-
flesh nose, plump-ripe fruit and exotic but trim finish in
the mouth; 12% alcohol.

GERMANY

**9 Dr Hermann Erdener Treppchen
Riesling Spätlese 2011** £11.99/£13.99
One of several Majestic wines from this estate at Erden
in the Mosel, reprising the good old days when parcels of
fine and usually well-aged German wines were a regular
feature in the stores. This is a very decent petrolly old
thing with elegant sweet-apple fruit, authentic Riesling
raciness and just 8% alcohol.

ITALY

8 Cortese Araldica 2019 £7.99/£8.99
Racy grassy-fresh but nuanced pale dry wine from
Piedmont, where the Cortese grape is mainly employed
in famed – and sometimes rather expensive – Gavi wines.
This is a nifty introduction at a sensible price; 12%
alcohol.

8 Passimento Bianco Pasqua 2019 £9.99/£11.99
Old friend at Majestic features a messy scribble-art label
giving little indication of what it is. In short, it's the white
equivalent of Valpolicella Ripasso, the plumped up red
wine of Verona now found in every supermarket. This is
in effect Soave, Verona's classic dry white, enriched with
wine from grapes concentrated under the sun to make
an exotic, creamy and fascinating dry wine of unique
character; 13% alcohol.

WHITE WINES

NEW ZEALAND

8 Yealands Estate Sauvignon Blanc 2019   £6.49/£10.49

Heavily discounted mix-six price was a draw but this stands up on quality grounds too. Bright gooseberry style vivid with leafy freshness and herb-garden aromas from a top Marlborough winery; 12.5% alcohol.

9 Waimea Estate Sauvignon Blanc 2017   £8.99/£12.99

'Grassy-gooseberry, super-zesty wine with massive lingering fruit and a nifty nettly finish', I enthused of the 2003 vintage of this Nelson, Marlborough classic in 2005. The 2017 vintage (13.5% alcohol) entirely complies, I'm pleased to report. And consider the price: £8.99 as part of your minimum mixed dozen in 2005 – and the same now in a mix-six. Who saw that coming?

SOUTH AFRICA

9 Definition Chenin Blanc 2019   £7.99/£12.99

Peaches and sweet pears, honey and blanched nuts balance with citrus twang and bright freshness in this artful Cape contrivance; 14% alcohol. One of the better items in Majestic's own-label Definition range.

8 Gabb Family Chardonnay 2019   £10.99/£14.99

Oaked Stellenbosch wine with old-fashioned appeal: creamy-peachy-melon fruit of comforting weight nicely poised by a discreet limey acidity; 13% alcohol.

SPARKLING WINES

8 Bouvet Ladubay Saumur Brut   £9.99/£13.99

Cracking Loire full-fizz sparkler made by what was once called the 'champagne method' before the champagne industry litigated the term out of existence, this is from the astoundingly versatile Chenin Blanc grape, making for nectary aromas and elegant orchard-citrus fruit flavours; 12.5% alcohol.

9 Heidsieck & Co Monopole Champagne Brut 2010 'Gold Top'   £22.99/£29.99

The 'Gold Top' branding might stir memories of the creamiest of doorstep-delivered milks and why not? This is a creamy champagne in its own way with gold colour, aromas of sweetly filled biscuits and a mellowness of fruit surely made all the more so by the passage of time since harvest a decade ago; 12.5% alcohol. A gift at the mix six price.

FRANCE

—Marks & Spencer—

How's this for dedication? I stood in a socially distanced queue outside the M&S Simply Food branch in Frome, Somerset – it's the nearest outlet to my home – for half an hour during a spectacular downpour, simply in quest of some of M&S's radical new wines. It was mid-June 2020 and I had only the day before discovered M&S had even launched these new wines.

The M&S at Frome, I'm sad to say, provided no kind of shelter for its patiently queuing customers. By the time I was allowed in, I was very wet and a bit cross. Let me just hope, I told myself, that this mission proves worthy of the journey, the discomforts and the expense. M&S's once-helpful press-relations office had told me nothing in advance about the retailer's plans for new wine ranges, so I didn't feel inclined to contact them in search of details. I'll find out about these wines for myself, I resolved. As if I were an ordinary customer rather than the consumer champion I like to believe I am.

So, in the pages to come, take my word for it: I'm giving you a thoroughly independent report. The few wines from the new ranges I bought and tried are here. The 13 simple wines are priced at £5, plus two sparklers at £6. They are labelled primarily with descriptive text such as 'Intense & Smooth' and seem to me to resemble the kind of wines you find gathering dust on the lower shelves of convenience stores. The new 'Classic' wines, on the other hand, look smart and interesting; they number about 35 and are being introduced progressively.

In the meantime, the regular M&S wine range is in flux. Gone are countless individual wines, many of them uniquely delicious, that have endured for decades. I am already missing them.

RED WINES

ARGENTINA

6 **This is … Bold & Velvety Malbec 2019**   £5.00
No mistaking the coffee/burnt toast Mendoza Malbec nose but it doesn't deliver in either boldness or velvetiness, too light and lean, even if 13.5% alcohol. Yes I know it's only a fiver, but if that's your budget, remember there are other places to shop.

AUSTRALIA

8 **This is … Rich & Spicy Shiraz 2019**   £5.00
Much better than the Mendoza Malbec above in that it delivers some of the way on heft and intensity; I wouldn't call it rich, but the Shiraz spice is evident and the weight is sufficient to satisfy; not bad for a fiver; 13.5% alcohol.

9 **Burra Brook Cabernet Sauvignon 2019**   £7.00
Perennial favourite on fine form is made as much in the restrained Bordeaux style as in the upfront Aussie mode but still generous with cassis ripeness and in artful balance; 14% alcohol. M&S's food pairing suggestions range from 'sausage and mash to Oriental-style duck pancakes'.

CHILE

8 **This is … Intense & Smooth
Cabernet Sauvignon 2019**   £5.00
This was my first taste from the 2020-launched M&S 'simplified' range, and I'll confess I was apprehensive. How can any retailer profit from £5 wines, let alone one at M&S's end of the market? Well, I can't answer that – no-one to talk to at M&S – but this Chilean red, one of a range of 15 different £5 wines (all right, the two sparklers are £6) proves the rule. It's not so much intense and smooth, more middleweight and acceptably mellow, but it's identikit Chilean Cabernet, perfectly wholesome, balanced and ripe (13% alcohol). I do hope the jaunty and highly unoriginal presentation style appeals to M&S customers.

RED WINES

🍷 9 **M&S Classics No. 11 Corbières 2019** £8.00

I feared this young wine would be hard and stringy, but not a bit of it. Youthful beetroot colour, but an easy brambly nose and warmly ripe sunny hedgerow fruits with appreciable intensity and the right garrigue spiciness; 13.5% alcohol. M&S recommend pairing it with 'rich and flavourful dishes with fresh herbs'.

🍷 8 **M&S Classics No.35 Beaujolais Villages 2019** £8.00

A wine of serious ripeness and heft (13.5% alcohol), and contrary to what M&S say, in my view this isn't the kind of Beaujolais you drink chilled (the ordinary wines are a treat from the fridge on the right occasions), but with menus including poultry and game, charcuterie or other cold cuts, or mushroom dishes for vegetarian/vegan options. Big, juicy and more purple in flavour than colour (it's unusually ruby, none of the usual blue tinge) it's a very respectable wine from Paul Sapin, who has supplied Beaujolais to M&S for ever, and seems to be involved in other aspects of the new ranges, too.

🍷 8 **Château Gillet 2018** £8.50

Ready-to-drink mid-weight Merlot-led claret has defined briar and black-cherry fruit flavours of wholesome charm; 13% alcohol. Bordeaux at this price level is not always like this. M&S claim it is 'ideal as a foil for delicately flavoured dishes such as roast chicken…or a nut roast'.

RED WINES

🍷 8 Paul Fontaine Coteaux Bourguignons 2018   £8.50

The appellation Coteaux Bourguignons replaced the former Bourgogne Grand Ordinaire a decade ago but wines under this new, more positive designation have really only just started to appear. This mix of Gamay and Pinot Noir has a cheery ruby-mauve colour, strawberry-raspberry juiciness and refreshing briskness; 13% alcohol.

🍷 8 Pinot Noir Pays d'Oc 2018   £8.50

From long-term M&S producer Domaine Mandeville a ripe generic Languedoc Pinot with more intensity of colour and fruit than you'd get from Burgundy at this sort of price; round and bouncy with mellow cherry fruit; 13% alcohol. A good match for meaty beef or lamb dishes, and will stand up to a little spice too.

🍷 8 Fleurie 2018   £10.00

I tasted this in 2019 and it's still on offer. I'm reprising it after saying it was quite sinewy and tense in its youth but should turn out quite special after a while in the bottle; fine juicy Beaujolais from a very good vintage; 13% alcohol.

RED WINES

🍷 10 M&S Classics No. 36 Bourgogne
Pinot Noir 2018 £12.00

One of my little collection from M&S's new 2020 ranges, and possibly the best of them. Healthy cherry colour, not too pale. Nose earthy, even farmyardy, with a wholesome raspiness – good counterpoint to pork – but in a wider context balanced in that way of sweet Burgundy Pinot fruit alongside abrasion. The main thing is its friendly juicy natural generosity (13% alcohol). Call it affordable Burgundy (probably Chalonnais), a reminder that there's still some of it left in the world and these guys have found it. I'm top-scoring it because it is just right.

🍷 9 Palatia Pinot Noir 2018 £9.00

Made by former M&S buyer Gerd Stepp in the Rheinpfalz/Palatinate, a light but lush raspberry-juicy, bouncing Pinot very much in its own, presumably German, style. It's elegant but long-flavoured and perfectly poised between lusciousness and gentle abrasion; 12.5% alcohol. Drink it cool as an aperitif or with poultry, game or cured meats.

🍷 10 El Duque de Miralta Rioja
Crianza 2015 £9.50

It's still on sale and even fractionally down in price (£10 last year), the entry-level wine in M&S's 2019-launched new Rioja range by serious bodega El Coto in the fab vintage of 2015. It's maturing beautifully, taking on a mellow orange hue and offering slinky vanilla-cassis richness in the fruit; 13.5% alcohol.

FRANCE

GERMANY

SPAIN

RED WINES

9 **El Duque de Miralta Rioja
Reserva 2014** £12.00

Next in the series by El Coto, a sweetly oaked and splendidly opaque cassis-and-spice wine of dark charm and silky textures; it stands out sufficiently to warrant the price; 13.5% alcohol.

8 **Rioja Tempranillo Perez
Burton 2017** £12.50

Unclassified Rioja is nevertheless smoothly oaked and silkily, spicily blackcurranty in the best traditions of the region; 14% alcohol. It's priced at the level of a *gran reserva* (well, a supermarket *gran reserva* in fairness) and is certainly of comparable quality even this young in bottle.

8 **El Duque de Miralta Rioja
Gran Reserva 2012** £15.00

I wondered last year if this senior wine in M&S's 2019-launched new Rioja range might be in need of a year or two longer in bottle to get where it should be going. Here's your chance to check on progress, as the vintage in question, the 2012, is still on sale. 'Dense, soupy rich colour and sweet violet-and-vanilla waft from this still-grippy long and deluxe wine', I noted; 13.5% alcohol.

PINK WINES

8 **La Dame en Rose Rosé 2019** £6.50

Liked the 2018 very much last year and assume the 2019 is in place. It's from the Midi and according to M&S winemaker Belinda Kleinig it's 'dry and fruity, a nod to Provence in the colour and taste, and very easy drinking'. A modest 11.5% alcohol and a modest price too.

SPAIN

FRANCE

PINK WINES

 Gold Label Rosé 2019 £7.00

Straight up, I'm assuming this old Languedoc friend will have made it into this vintage and that it matches the 2018 for jolly cerise colour and fruit evocations ranging from rose-hip to crisp redcurrant; 11.5% alcohol.

WHITE WINES

 Gold Label Chardonnay Pays d'Oc 2018 £7.00

Old-fashioned brand (I'm surprised not to see 'St Michael' somewhere in the name) with old-fashioned virtues of sunny colour, sweet-apple Chardonnay nose clear as a bell and proper Mediterranean ripeness running through the peachy fruit; 12.5% alcohol. The 2019 can't be far behind.

 M&S Classics No. 1 Bourgogne Chardonnay 2018 £8.00

'Vibrant, fresh and modern', says the back label. Perhaps I could add that it has the less-modern attributes of fine lemon-gold colour, cheery cabbage nose and friendly melon ripeness, though not at all overripe. A small proportion of the blend has been aged in oak barrel, I gather. Well-presented wine, presumably Mâconnais, for a very fair price (for Burgundy); 12.5% alcohol.

WHITE WINES

 9 Côte de Charme Sauvignon Blanc 2019 £9.00

Mystery wine from the Loire Valley, as easy to like as its alluring name: bright greengage-grassy aroma, layered Sauvignon fruit flavours embracing customary asparagus, gooseberries and blackcurrant leaf and with a memorable intensity alongside the pebbly freshness; 11.5% alcohol.

 8 Chablis 2018 £12.00

It was nostalgic to try this again after so many years (can't remember it from any recent tastings) and to see the label design hasn't altered in what seems like decades. Fine gunflinty wine by dependable Cave des Vignerons co-op, and it's authentic, crisp and generous with ripe Chardonnay fruit in the famous appellation's inimitable style; 12.5% alcohol.

 10 M&S Classics No. 2 Mineralstein Riesling Pfalz 2019 £9.50

Sumptuous but restrained and elegant Rhine Riesling of great quality and character by former M&S staffer Gerd Stepp from his ancestral vineyards in the Palatinate. This is a food wine (we had potted shrimp, scotch egg, salami, raw carrots and Portuguese cakes but anything else would have done) of infinite possibility. It is indeed minerally, and jumps with orchard fruit, owing something to the Alsace style, I thought; 12% alcohol.

WHITE WINES

8 Garganega Pinot Grigio 2018   £7.00

ITALY

The prime mover in this Veneto dry wine is the Garganega (85% of the mix), the Soave grape – and it does indeed closely resemble the style of that famous Verona vino, with brassica green freshness counterpointed by fleeting blanched-almond creaminess all en route to a keen citrus finish; 12.5% alcohol.

8 Craft 3 Marlborough Sauvignon Blanc 2018   £10.00

NEW ZEALAND

The 2019 is expected but meantime relish the healthy silage pong from this grassy, racy and long-flavoured seafood matcher; 13% alcohol.

8 Saint Clair James Sinclair Sauvignon Blanc 2019   £15.00

Big flavours from a famous Marlborough estate encompass classic Kiwi Sauvignon notes of asparagus and gooseberry, seagrass and nettles all in cohesive balance, quite delicious, necessary at the price; 13% alcohol.

5 This is …Ripe & Juicy Fruity White 2019   £5.00

SPAIN

'Medium Sweet White Wine', it says as the subtitle to this sugary generic, which smells quite inviting with its peachy-melon allure but cloys in the mouth and certainly disappointed me; 10.5%. I'm mentioning it because I handed over £5 for it, please indulge me.

SPARKLING WINES

FRANCE

🍷 8 **Champagne Delacourt Brut** £25.00
New house champagne launched in 2018 is as good as
ever and £5 cheaper. It's pleasingly mellow with crisp
red-apple fruit and lasting flavours; 12.5% alcohol.

🍷 8 **Champagne Delacourt Medium Dry** £25.00
It is, I guess, the same base champagne as the one above,
only with a bit more *dosage*, the sugar-wine mix added at
the time of the disgorgement. Here the effect is to soften
as much as to sweeten the finished champagne, taking
some of the greenness out of it. If you don't like your
fizz too edgy this might well be the one for you; 12.5%
alcohol.

Morrisons

What a loss the Morrisons tasting has been. It's been held in the last few years in a novel venue: the top floor of Foyles bookshop in London's Charing Cross Road. As a rule there are a couple of hundred wines on taste, and we scribblers can get a genuinely broad picture of this company's continuously improving range. While doing this, we can also enjoy some music. The great airy room has space not only for all those echelons of wine, but for a grand piano too, and a virtuoso musician to play it.

Even the most hard-bitten critics have been known to hum along to the tunes, and occasionally requests are made. A young woman player once obliged me with an uplifting keyboard rendition of *The Girl from Ipanema*.

But I digress. Obviously, I have tasted very many fewer Morrisons wines in the run-up to this year's edition. But it has been a pleasure to pop into the store, socially distanced queues notwithstanding, to buy the wines for this report. I have cautiously stuck to new vintages of wines I already knew, with just a few adventures further afield, and I continue to be convinced that Morrisons is making steady progress.

RED WINES

ARGENTINA

9 **The Best Gran Montaña Malbec 2019** £7.75
From top Mendoza producer Catena, a delightful, velvety varietal (there's a bit of Cabernet in the mix) combining generous blackberry intensity with Malbec sinew and spice into a thoroughly savoury whole; 13.5% alcohol.

8 **Viñalba Patagonia Malbec 2018** £10.00
Gamey savour to this dark and spicy blend with Syrah grapes sits well with the smooth texture from oak contact; 14.5% alcohol.

AUSTRALIA

8 **The Best Margaret River Shiraz 2018** £7.50
You get a lot of plumptious sweet-spicy, even toffee-rich, but balanced and clean-finishing classic Shiraz fruit (there's one-eighth Merlot here too) in this friendly monster from Western Australia; 14.5% alcohol.

CHILE

9 **Morrisons Merlot 2019** £4.50
Marvellous party red from user-friendly grape variety exploited to the full for juicy black-cherry plumpness and ripeness, artfully balanced with discreet acidity; 13% alcohol.

8 **The Best Chilean Carmenère 2019** £7.75
Creamily oaked but brightly juicy bramble-cassis fruit in this distinctive Rapel Valley wine of very attractive carmine colour – source of the grape's name; 13.5% alcohol.

RED WINES

10 Raoul Clerget Beaujolais 2019 £5.00
Exemplary purple bouncy-juicy everyday Beaujolais of
lively character to drink cool. It's joyously juicy and has a
proper grip of healthy tannin at the finish; 13% alcohol.
Raoul Clerget is a brand name of Les Grands Chais de
France, one of the leading suppliers of French wines
to supermarkets throughout the world. LGC bought
Clerget, a biggish Burgundy producer and merchant, five
years ago and has somehow managed to maintain the
quality of this very decent wine. I think it's the best-value
everyday Beaujolais on the market, pound for pound.

8 The Best Côtes Catalanes 2017 £7.75
Found this on promo at £6, which was good value for
a gripping garrigue winter warmer of likeable roundness
and savour; 14% alcohol. It's from the wild country just
north of the Pyrenees, France's mountainous frontier
with Spain's Catalonia.

8 The Best Languedoc 2017 £7.75
I scored the 2016 wine 10 in the 2020 edition and urge
readers to try the 2017 – which is more than I have been
able to do locally, I must admit. A reminder of my note
on the 2016: 'amazing contrivance has dense, mellowing
colour, wild garrigue aromas and sleek spiciness ...
13.5% alcohol'.

8 Vinus Paul Mas Malbec 2017 £8.25
Still in stock from last year, a Languedoc riposte to the
Argentine model of Malbec by leading Midi wine mogul
Jean Claude Mas has deep inky colour, spicy-smoky nose
and intense blackberry fruit with hallmark roasty savour;
13.5% alcohol.

FRANCE

RED WINES

FRANCE

8 **Cairanne Le Verdier Cru des Côtes du Rhône J. Boulard 2018** £10.00
Big handsome wine from lately promoted individual southern Rhône village *cru* is darkly spicy with a liquorice twist and long flavours; 14.5% alcohol. I paid £8 on promo.

8 **Sorso Montepulciano 2018** £6.75
This boldly-branded screwtop Abruzzo party wine has plenty of juicy ripeness (13% alcohol) and hedgerow-fruit bounce for pasta nights. Up in price from £6.00 last year but I paid just £5.00 on promo.

ITALY

9 **The Best Barbera d'Asti 2017** £7.50
The unassuming label undersells this delicious bouncy-but-gutsy bramble and briar Piedmont pasta wine by ubiquitous regional giant Araldica; 14.5% alcohol and if anything even better on second opening. Price is up £1 on last year's 2016 vintage.

8 **The Best Primitivo 2018** £7.50
Pleasingly dark and savoury Puglian wine has the right baked flavours and wholesome heft that mark out the distinctive Primitivo style; 13.5% alcohol.

9 **The Best Nerello Mascalese 2018** £7.75
Jazzy presentation for this big, juicy blueberry-pruny food red from Sicily, generously ripe in this vintage with 13.5% alcohol and a brisk finish. Impressive and satisfying from one of the island's most distinctive indigenous grapes. These wines can age very gracefully.

RED WINES

ITALY

🍷 9 **The Best Toscana 2018** £9.00
Made for Morrisons at San Felice, a Chianti Classico estate
near Siena; an experimental blend of local Sangiovese
with Cabernet Sauvignon, Merlot and other non-Chianti
grapes to make a 'supertuscan blend of luscious, intense
and thoroughly Tuscan character'; but it's not Chianti;
12.5% alcohol.

🍷 8 **Fontanafredda Barolo 2014** £22.00
I tasted this vintage in 2019, loved it even at the
outrageous price and commended in this space last
time out. It's stocked in only 100 Morrisons branches
and might well take years to sell out. I commend it
still for its limpid charms, authentic spirity tar'n'roses
perfume and sleek, powerful but courtly flavours;
13.5% alcohol.

PORTUGAL

🍷 6 **The Best Douro 2017** £7.50
Hmm. Made by generic giant Falua, a sinewy, dare I say
stringy, wine with some porty savour, but not much;
13.5% alcohol. The 2016 vintage last year was a triumph,
so maybe this is just a glitch. I paid £6 on promo, but that
was still too much.

SOUTH AFRICA

🍷 8 **The Best Fairtrade Cabernet
Sauvignon 2019** £7.25
Fresh even leafy wholesome Cabernet from the Swartland
has easy-spicy blackcurranty fruit and a notion of
creaminess, I assume from some oak contact, 13.5%
alcohol.

RED WINES

8 Carta Roja Jumilla 2019   £7.75

Sinewy dark steak-and-chips red, almost raisiny in its ripeness and savour, but by no means overcooked; memorable style and plenty of poke at 14.5% alcohol. I've seen this discounted to £6 – and that's a bargain.

9 The Best Priorat 2016   £10.00

This is the same vintage I raved about last year. Why on earth hasn't it sold out? Snap it up while you can. Authentic pungent-silky elegant midweight from exotic Catalan backwater at an unusually approachable price: I paid £8.00 on promo; 14.5% alcohol.

**8 The Best Marques de Los Rios
Rioja Reserva 2014**   £10.00

Plausible if pricy tobacco-strawberry maturing soft red with recognisable style; don't be put off by the gaudy livery; 13.5% alcohol.

PINK WINES

**8 L'Escarpe Coteaux d'Aix en
Provence Rosé 2019**   £8.75

Delicate pale shell-pink colour in the Provence manner, discreet redcurrant/floral nose and matching elusive but refreshing dry fruit flavours finishing brisk; 12.5% alcohol. The best of a surprisingly limited choice of Provence pinks at Morrisons.

8 Vitis Nostra Pinot Noir Rosé 2019   £7.25

Good coral colour and the strawberry-cherry aromas you'd expect from a Pinot Noir wine; dry and bright and convincing; 11.5% alcohol. Look for a £10 for two bottles promo.

SPAIN

FRANCE

ITALY

Morrisons

WHITE WINES

ARGENTINA

🍷 9 **The Best Uco Valley Gran Montaña**
Chardonnay 2017 £8.75

Still the same vintage as last year, and it's ageing gracefully, a successful tilt by excellent La Agricola winery in the Andean province of Mendoza at the Burgundy style of Chardonnay, this is succulently ripe and rich but with clear minerality and citrus twang to balance; oaked but brightly fresh and stimulating and jolly good value; 13% alcohol.

AUSTRALIA

🍷 8 **Workshop Bench Blend**
Chardonnay 2019 £6.75

This Yeoman unoaked modern peach-and-apple fresh varietal is wholesome and balanced; 12% alcohol.

🍷 8 **The Best Western Australia**
Chardonnay 2018 £8.00

I suspect the 2019 will be along any minute, but liked the 2018's nostalgic note of sweet vanilla lushness in the otherwise bracingly fresh mineral white-peach fruit; 13% alcohol.

CHILE

🍷 8 **The Best Chilean Chardonnay 2019** £7.25

Steady perennial from Casablanca producer Cono Sur has full ripe peachy-melon fruit (13.5% alcohol) and a tidy crisp finish; unoaked but not without a little lusciousness.

WHITE WINES

CHILE

🍷 **8** **Cono Sur Bicicleta Viognier 2019**   £7.50
Viognier is a balancing act, rather like riding a bicycle. To work, the wine needs to integrate the natural apricot and mango sweetness of the grape with the counterpointing lemon-lime acidity it can impart. This one does it just right: it's lush and fresh, long and crisp; 13% alcohol. The bicycle theme of the package, incidentally, here refers to the sustainable practices of the Cono Sur vineyards. Workers ride bikes rather than travelling in trucks or cars, and the vines are kept free of weeds and pests by a flock of more than 1,000 geese.

FRANCE

🍷 **8** **Pomerols Picpoul de Pinet 2019**   £8.00
Understandably popular seafood wine made near the Mediterranean resort of Sète; perky, crisp and fleetingly saline, a nice introduction to the style; 13% alcohol. This has been on promo at £6.50.

🍷 **9** **The Best Alsace Pinot Gris 2018**   £8.50
Very pleased to see Morrisons are continuing with this mildly esoteric but magnificently flavoured Alsace wine. It illustrates perfectly the yawning gap between the ethereal Italian style of PG (Pinot Grigio) and the French. This has rich colour, smoky autumnal-fruit lushness and keen lifting limey acidity; fascinating as an aperitif and, inevitably, an oft-recommended match for Asian food flavours; 13% alcohol.

Morrisons

WHITE WINES

9 **The Best Vouvray 2018** £8.75
Distinguished Loire appellation makes lush white wines ranging in style from dry to *moelleux* ('marrowy' sweet). This one is off-dry with honeysuckle nose, sweet peachy white fruit lifted by clear citrus zest, making a truly exotic balance of flavour; 12.5% alcohol. It's made from Chenin Blanc grapes, a fine aperitif and a versatile match for shellfish as well as white meats and interesting cheeses.

9 **The Best Pouilly Fumé 2019** £12.00
The Best Sauvignon, they used to say, comes from the central Loire Valley and in particular from two riverside towns, Sancerre and Pouilly-sur-Loire. Sancerre tends to top Pouilly-Fumé (as Pouilly likes to style its wines) in price, but the jury's always out on true quality. This is a very decent one, glitteringly, pebbly fresh and long with grassy, nettly lush green flavours and limey edginess; 12.5% alcohol.

9 **The Best Chablis 1er Cru 2015** £15.00
Well, Morrisons said they still have this outstanding vintage – which scored 9 here last year – so see if you can find it as Chablis of this quality only gets better and better in its first few years. This one has authentic gold-shot-with-green colour, flinty Chardonnay fruit and a lick of richness from partial blending of oak-matured wine; 13% alcohol.

WHITE WINES

ITALY

8 **The Best Falanghina 2019** **£7.00**

From the Campania, the countryside of Naples, a clean bright very dry white with a note of quince among the fruit evocations; works for me; 13% alcohol.

8 **The Best Gavi 2019** **£8.00**

Currently cool Piedmont wine by regional giant Araldica has its own herbaceous appeal in aroma and flavour equally, giving distinction to the crisp white orchard fruit; 12.5% alcohol.

9 **Minea Greco di Tufo 2018** **£8.75**

Smart package for an intriguing and rather wonderful wine. Greco is the grape, so-named because it possibly descends from vines imported into southern Italy by Greek settlers centuries BCE. Tufo is a village of the Campania where today's vines flourish in volcanic soils that might just inoculate the wine with a brimstone spiciness. This is a richly coloured wine, fresh and crisp and showing the lovely Jaffa-orange acidity that typifies the style; 12.5% alcohol.

NEW ZEALAND

8 **The Best Marlborough Sauvignon Blanc 2019** **£8.25**

Made by the much-admired Yealands Estate, this is a proper fruit and veg stall of a Sauvignon. Aromas and flavours embrace green pepper, mangetout (honestly), asparagus and, natch, gooseberries. In the round it all works cohesively into a fascinating and refreshing whole; 12.5% alcohol.

WHITE WINES

SOUTH AFRICA

8 **The Best South African Sauvignon Blanc 2019** £6.75
Stellenbosch wine has trademark Cape grapefruity Sauvignon style, and a good heft of grassy lushness; works well at a good price; 12.5% alcohol.

9 **The Best Chenin Blanc 2019** £7.50
Honeysuckle nose meets crisp orchard fruit in this wonderfully balanced Swartland wine full of freshness and ripeness in blissful harmony; 13.5% alcohol. South African Chenin is the white wine to watch.

8 **Kleine Zalze Chenin Blanc 2019** £7.50
I am stricken by the absence of possible stablemate Klein Street Grenache Blanc which top-scored in this space in the 2020 edition. It seems to have been dropped. In consolation try this easy, fresh new apple-peach-melon contrivance (13% alcohol) and hope for a return of the Grenache.

SPAIN

10 **The Best Marques de Los Rios Rioja Blanca Reserva 2016** £13.00
Worthy successor to the terrific 2015 vintage of this unreconstructed relic from Rioja's near-extinguished past as a producer of utterly distinctive richly oaky white wines of wonderfully oxidative character; it's pure gold in colour and vanilla-lush opulence but keenly edgy and bright; an absolute joy; 12% alcohol.

FORTIFIED WINES

SPAIN

 8 **Morrisons Fino Sherry** £5.75

Sadly Morrisons seem to have dropped their connection with Jerez producer Lustau, and the new sherry range is just not the same. This fino, very pale and dry (just as the label intimates) is perfectly good for serving very chilled; 15% alcohol.

Sainsbury's

 I have found nearly 50 wines to recommend from Sainsbury's. Some of them appeared in this space last year because they are non-vintage – sparkling wines for example – and some are still on shelf from last year's vintage. Most of the wines are those I have bought in my local, well-stocked store during the long hot summer of 2020.

Perhaps I shouldn't mention this, but the socially distanced queues in which I have found myself at Sainsbury's have been by a mile (well, maybe that's an exaggeration) the longest in time and space of any I have had to endure at a supermarket. I suppose it's a tribute to the loyalty and persistence of Sainsbury's customers, as well as to the undoubted appeal of Sainsbury's merchandise.

All but a handful of the wines I've featured are from Sainsbury's Taste the Difference (TTD) range. This does not signify that these are the only wines worth buying; rather it indicates that TTD wines with which I am already acquainted are the safest bet for me to buy, try and report upon for these pages. Just for comparison, in last year's *Best Wines in the Supermarkets*, after tasting a wide range of brands as well as own-brand wines at Sainsbury's London HQ, I commended 65 Sainsbury's wines – all but a handful of them TTD.

RED WINES

Sainsbury's

ARGENTINA

♍ 9 Taste the Difference Morador Malbec 2018   £7.50

The 2019 will follow but I haven't tasted it, but must include this fine Fairtrade wine from last year's edition as I scored it 10. It's a classic dark roasty-spicy Andean pure Malbec with oak contact and black savour; 13.5% alcohol. Price has fallen from £8.50 to £7.50 perhaps in line with the collapse of Argentina's economic fortunes. I've dropped the score by just one point because I doubt the 2018 will still be on shelf – but maybe the 2019 will surpass it.

FRANCE

♍ 9 Taste the Difference Languedoc 2018   £7.00

Don't infer from the dependability of this hardy annual that it is in any way predictable. This vintage is another triumph for Jean-Claude's Mas's Grenache Syrah Carignan blend with generous ripeness (13.5% alcohol), spicy briar black fruits smoothed with a proportion of oak-held wine and a healthy tannic grip. Price has held at this bargain level for years, with occasional promos to £6.50.

♍ 8 Taste the Difference Saint Chinian 2017   £9.00

There's a distinct fruits-of-the-forest savour to this singular Mediterranean red. I very much like the abrasive spicy-garriguey briary fruit and its firm tannic grip (14.5% alcohol) but concede it might be an acquired taste.

RED WINES

FRANCE

♈ 9 **Brouilly Georges Duboeuf 2017** £9.50
The floral label decorations and white screwtops on 'King
of Beaujolais' Georges Duboeuf's range are consistently
impressive. Same goes for the quality and authenticity of
the wines, with delicious renderings of each appellation
plus the ten crus of Beaujolais. This Brouilly is delightfully
juicy and bright, but silkily nuanced and contemplative
too; 13% alcohol. Beaujolais wines by Georges Duboeuf
(1933–2020) are very widely stocked in the better kind of
supermarkets and are remarkably consistent for quality.
Value seems pretty fair to me – Beaujolais *crus* can
sometimes look overpriced – but Duboeuf wines are very
frequently discounted in-store.

♈ 8 **Taste the Difference Pic St Loup 2017** £11.00
No sign of the 2018 before deadline, but if you do find
the 2017 it might well be a better wine than it was when
I tasted it a year ago – 'spicily dark and briary, maybe a
bit sinewy, distinctively relishable but in need of time'.
I have high hopes of the 2018 turning out to equal the
10-scoring 2016. Take the plunge.

♈ 9 **Taste the Difference Château Les**
   Bouysses Cahors Malbec 2016 £13.00
Haven't tasted the 2017 but I'm so taken with the
previous vintage (I bought six and have a couple left)
that I'll dare to assume the 2016 is still out there. It's a
proper Cahors, bible black (well, nearly), bulging with
blackberry fruit, rich but spiky, creamy but juicy, joyfully
ripe and balanced; 13.5% alcohol.

RED WINES

FRANCE

🍷 8 **Louis Max Côte de Nuits**
Villages 2018   **£19.00**

I've been eyeing this wine for years, passing reluctantly by the premium section in various Sainsbury's wine departments, deterred by the price – alarming for a generic burgundy – but now I've tasted the new 2018 vintage (not from Sainsbury's, who have never offered it for tasting as far as I know) and must report it is silkily delicious, lively with juicy Pinot Noir raspberry-cherry ripeness and worthy of bottle age; 13% alcohol. Burgundophiles can invest with confidence.

ITALY

🍷 9 **Taste the Difference Valpolicella**
Ripasso 2017   **£11.00**

Warm black-cherry base to the intense fruit of this speciality Veronese is highlighted with notions of bitter chocolate, coffee, even prune. It's not sweet, it's rich, and a great match for cheese as well as highly flavoured meat dishes; 14% alcohol. Every supermarket now does a ripasso, and this one stands out.

🍷 8 **Taste the Difference Barbaresco 2014**   **£11.00**

Cautionary note: the latest vintage I've tasted is the 2014 which looked pale and seemed underweight but had, I thought, prospects of development. Some years have been brillo (eg 2010) and some much less so; if you find the 2015 on sale, I'd risk it.

RED WINES

PORTUGAL

🍷 9   **Taste the Difference Lisboa 2018**   £7.00
Lisboa as a wine region is the hilly landscape surrounding
the capital city. Red wines from Castelão grapes (among
others) dominate, and this is a good one: sleek and dark
with hallmark Portuguese clove and cinnamon spiciness,
it has definition and balance; 13.5% alcohol.

🍷 8   **Taste the Difference Douro 2017**   £10.50
Big flavoured port-nosed winter warmer by the
ubiquitous Symington family; has the right blackberry-
elderberry intensity for a Douro table wine with plenty of
woof (14.5% alcohol). Last one I tasted, the 2015, from
Quinta do Crasto, was more exciting.

🍷 8   **Feuerheed's Anchor Wine 2017**   £11.00
Novelty wine in a paper wrapper complete with gift tag
('A handmade gift for ... from ...') for you to fill in before
handover. It proved irresistible to me and wasn't as bad
as I'd expected: a weighty Douro red with porty darkness
and spice, pruny and plump from oak contact and 13.5%
alcohol.

SOUTH AFRICA

🍷 9   **Taste the Difference South African
Pinotage 2019**   £7.50
Plushly textured typically savoury densely piquant
red-meat matcher from the Cape's indigenous grape.
Fairtrade-made, and very fair value too. Pinotage can be
a bit stewed but this one shines for purity of flavour and
wholesome balance; 14% alcohol.

RED WINES

Sainsbury's

SPAIN

8 Carta Roja Grand Reservada
Monastrell 2016 £5.75

I fear unwary shoppers might mistake this gaudily liveried item for Rioja. It is in fact from Jumilla, a Valencian backwater renowned for robust and spicy dark red wines from Monastrell grapes – nothing in common with Rioja at all. But I liked this macho bargain a lot, and commend it with spicy-meaty menus, Spanish or otherwise; 13.5% alcohol.

9 Taste the Difference Navarra 2018 £7.00

I've long been a fan of this bold blackberry-blueberry regional classic, but have lately realised Sainsbury's never include it in their tastings, so here it is at last. Navarra is a historic region of Spain overshadowed in viticultural terms by its neighbour Rioja, and making robust, rich reds that deserve more attention. This one is mostly Garnacha, muscular but silky, a great match for roast meats; 13.5% alcohol.

9 Taste the Difference Rioja Viñedos
Barrihuelo Crianza 2017 £7.75

Beguiling creamy midweight wine has lively even youthful juicy blackcurrant fruit; a perky but not unserious spin on the eternal Rioja theme; 13.5% alcohol. You can also buy single-serve 187ml bottles of this wine for £2.50 a pop.

8 Taste the Difference Cepa Alegro
Rioja Reserva 2014 £9.00

Sweet vanilla and cassis fruit in pretty good balance in this safe, consistent Rioja from an underwhelming vintage in the region; 13.5% alcohol.

RED WINES

9 **Taste the Difference Priorat 2017** £12.00

I accept that it looks expensive, as a generic wine, at £12 but the sequestered enclave of Priorat in Catalonia is one of the world's most exalted vineyard hotspots, with corresponding prices. This one (for which I paid a mere £10 on promo) is a fine introduction to the style: opaque appearance, luxuriant blackcurrant-concentrate aromas with notes of liquorice (guess what: Priorat's slaty soil is known as *licorella*), mulberry, cocoa, and succulent luscious black-fruit flavours lushed up with vanilla, all in grand balance; 14.5% alcohol.

9 **Condado de Haza Crianza 2015** £15.00

The winery was established in 1989 by Tinta Pesquera, the producer that put Ribera del Duero on the map (*pace* Vega Sicilia) to make typical regional wines at untypically approachable prices. Even at £15 this is very fair value: blood-red colour, creamy texture conveying intense cassis, minty, spicy luscious fruits of opulent weight; it's gorgeous but not over the top; 14% alcohol. Occasionally offered on promo – be vigilant.

SPAIN

PINK WINES

8 **Taste the Difference Fronton
Negrette Rosé 2019** £7.00

Dry wine from the little-known Negrette grape of the Frontonnais near Toulouse has a good coral colour and sweet strawberry nose; fresh and delicately flavourful with 12.5% alcohol.

FRANCE

PINK WINES

🍷 8 **Taste the Difference Côtes de Provence Rosé 2019** £9.75

Nicely presented coppery-hued, florally scented Mediterranean wine is safely dry but delivers plenty of sunny strawberry-redcurrant flavours; 12.5% alcohol.

🍷 8 **Les Caillottes Sancerre Rosé 2019** £13.00

Now that decent Provence rosé has typically climbed close to £10, posh pinks like Sancerre look more worth a punt. This pure Pinot Noir has a fine bright hue, proper cherry-raspberry nose and matching brisk even crunchy fresh fruit; 13% alcohol.

WHITE WINES

🍷 9 **Taste the Difference Barossa Chardonnay 2019** £7.00

It's made for Sainsbury's by dependable Chateau Tanunda (est 1890) and has held this £7 price for years, so it's a progressively growing bargain: peachy-lush part-oaked fruit with a fine natural minerality and citrus spike; great balance and 12.5% alcohol.

🍷 8 **Taste the Difference Grüner Veltliner 2019** £8.50

Agreeably spicy but briskly dry, it has the correct preserved-fruit aromas that distinguish GV as a particularly suitable aperitif wine and make it a good match for exotic and spicy menus; 12.5% alcohol.

WHITE WINES

 **Taste the Difference Austrian
Riesling 2019** £8.75
Bracing, crisp and yet ripely appley dry Riesling with
heady aromatics, this is a fine aperitif wine as well as an
obvious match for Asian dishes; 12.5% alcohol.

 **Taste the Difference Bordeaux
Sauvignon Blanc 2019** £7.00
Bordeaux's traditional dry whites have been rather left
behind in the Sauvignon Blanc boom. Here's a contender:
elegant pure restrained classic style with plenty of natural
Sauvignon character; 12.5% alcohol.

 **La Couronne des Plantagenets
Vouvray 2018** £7.25
Long-serving Sainsbury's exclusive from the Loire Valley
is just-dry but honeysuckle-scented, fresh and floral with
lush but appley white fruits; a style very well worth
discovery as an aperitif or as a versatile match for tricky
menus including salads and cured meats or fish; 11.5%
alcohol.

 **Taste the Difference Languedoc
Blanc 2019** £7.50
Totally consistent perennial by Mediterranean magician
Jean-Claude Mas is perfectly poised between exotic
ripeness and bright white-fruit flavours, leesy and long but
tangily crisp; 13% alcohol. Top value and yet regularly
discounted.

WHITE WINES

9 Taste the Difference Côtes du Rhône Blanc 2019 £8.00

White Côtes du Rhône is one of the undiscovered wonders of France's warm south, overshadowed by the entirely warranted renown of the region's red wines. Hats off to Sainsbury's for introducing this delicious and consistent example, produced by enterprising Gabriel Meffre, a few years back, and sticking with it. Plushly peachy and ripe, it's concocted from the classic regional blend of Grenache Blanc, Roussanne and Viognier grapes (the recipe for fabulously expensive white Châteauneuf du Pape), with some of the blend aged in oak casks. Fine floral-nectar aromas, nectarine and citrus acidity, crisp finishing, dry and bright; 12.5% alcohol.

8 Plaimont Côtes de Gascogne Colombard Sauvignon Blanc 2019 £8.00

Honeysuckle and acacia – the textbook aromas of warm-weather whites from Colombard grapes – are to the fore in this zesty and bright Gers dry blend with Sauvignon to offer lots of fresh orchard fruit lushness en route to a limey flavour edge; 11.5% alcohol.

8 Taste the Difference Muscadet de Sevre et Maine Sur Lie 2019 £8.00

Made from a grape variety called Melon de Bourgogne, this bone-dry Loire oyster-matcher tastes nothing like melon and even less like burgundy. But it's great: demandingly bracing and green yet lush and intense in its rush of tangy freshness, citrus at the rim, long on seaside savours; 12% alcohol.

WHITE WINES

🍷 9 Taste the Difference Gaillac
Blanc 2019   £8.00

Crisp Toulouse dry white. You get a fine lemon-gold colour, granny-smith-apple, brassica-citrus aroma and refreshing zest from a grape previously unknown to me, the Loin d'oeil; 12% alcohol. Discovered and enjoyed on a rare and responsibly social-distanced outhouse visit on an inclement summer evening. Thank you, Peter and Suzie.

🍷 9 Taste the Difference Petit
Chablis 2018   £10.50

I really took to the 2018 and had hoped to try the 2019, but no luck. If this is still on shelf, go for it – there is real Chablis character here: gunflint savour, wild Chardonnay freshness and slaking minerality; 12% alcohol. If the 2019 turns up, *tant mieux*!

🍷 10 Taste the Difference Pouilly
Fumé 2019   £13.00

Shimmering pure Sauvignon Blanc with the suitably river-fresh coolness and tang you expect from the famed shoreside vineyards of Pouilly-sur-Loire. A notion of smokiness in the flavour, perhaps conjured from the name Pouilly-Fumé. This own-brand, an early pioneer by Sainsbury's, is the real thing, a match for most of the grand individual estates of the appellation and a great buy at this price; 13% alcohol.

FRANCE

WHITE WINES

Sainsbury's

GERMANY

🍷 8 **Winemakers' Selection Riesling 2017**   £5.25
Soft but balanced Rheinhessen wine has the right mix of crisp-apple Riesling zest and retained delicate sweetness – it's just 9% alcohol. Price looks keen. If 2018 or 2019 vintage succeeds this, take it on trust.

🍷 8 **Taste the Difference German
Pinot Blanc 2019**   £7.75
Rheinpfalz spin on the theme of Alsace Pinot Blanc is a distinctive mix of aromatic and tangy with a little bit of white-nut creaminess; likeable herbaceous style with 13% alcohol. Pinot Blanc is usually called Weissburgunder in Germany.

ITALY

🍷 8 **Taste the Difference Pinot Grigio
Trentino 2019**   £7.00
If you insist on Italian PG, it might as well be this one. It's from the sub-Alpine Trentino region, where higher altitude might just make for more suitable fruit, and you get some of the smoke and aromatics that mark out Alsace PG; it's full of fruit and pretty dry; 12.5% alcohol.

🍷 8 **Taste the Difference Vernaccia di
San Gimignano 2019**   £8.00
Peculiar as it is to the many-towered Tuscan hill town, I wonder if this wine sells mostly to bewitched visitors to San Gimignano. Eschew the crowds and evoke the glories of the place by trying this briskly lemony refresher for its generous but defined white fruits; 12.5% alcohol.

WHITE WINES

ITALY

10 **Taste the Difference Greco
di Tufo 2018** £8.50

To my amazement, the price of this spiffy wine has fallen to £8.50 from £10 during 2020. Bravissimo! It's from a grape called Greco (imported by invading Greeks two millennia back) and grown in vineyards of volcanic tufo soil high in the ageless hills of the Campania south of Naples. It's dry, complex wine with suggestions not just of the wild flora that flourish on the surface but of the primordial mineralities of what lies beneath; 12.5% alcohol. Attractively presented, and a reliable food match even for assertive flavours.

9 **Taste the Difference Vermentino 2017** £9.00

Vermentino is a staple white-wine grape of Corsica and Sardinia, but this one is from Salice Salentino in Puglia; alluring rich colour and inviting floral aromas lead on to ripe orchard-fruit flavours of real resonance; very likeable, very Italian dry white to match all sorts of pastas and fowl as well as fishy dishes; 12.5% alcohol.

8 **Taste the Difference Gavi di Gavi 2019** £12.00

Serious Piedmontese dry white by local giant Araldica is worthy of the name (and price) – Gavi is cool, and Gavi di Gavi is ubercool – opulent in colour, wildly aromatic with orchard fruits, whitecurrants and citrus zests, intense with crisp but lush white fruit flavours and long, complex, and tinglingly fresh; 12.5% alcohol.

Sainsbury's

WHITE WINES

NEW ZEALAND

🍷 8 Taste the Difference Coolwater
Bay Sauvignon Blanc 2019   £8.00
Vivid crisp nettle-patch classic Marlborough wine seems especially ripe and developed in this vintage (no doubt soon to be displaced by the 2020, which I haven't tasted) delivering a lot of seagrassy savour; 12.5% alcohol.

PORTUGAL

🍷 8 Taste the Difference Portuguese
Alvarinho 2019   £7.50
A transparent attempt to exploit the craze for Spain's Rias Baixas Albariño, made just the other side of Portugal's northwest frontier, this has a steely nose and flavour with plenty of briny Atlantic freshness; better bet than vinho verde; 12.5% alcohol.

SPAIN

🍷 8 Taste the Difference Viñedos
Barrihuelo Rioja Blanco 2019   £7.00
Modern-style unoaked dry white Rioja by giant bodega Muriel shows off constituent grape Viura's hot-house-peach-style ripeness and juiciness to good effect with a twang of citrus to balance; 13% alcohol.

🍷 9 Taste the Difference Albariño
Rias Baixas 2019   £8.50
Sainsbury's was first among the supermarkets on to the Albariño bandwagon 20 years ago, and this wine has been out front ever since. It's blowing a proper Atlantic breeze of tangy salinity but also delivering generously ripened grassy fruit and lemon zest; 13.5% alcohol.

SPARKLING WINES

8 Taste the Difference Crémant de
Loire Rosé Brut   £11.50
Perky full-sparkler with attractive smoked-salmon colour
delivers a strawberry perfume in front of fresh, brisk
corresponding fruits. This is not at all like pink champagne
but a very fun fizz just the same; 12.5% alcohol.

10 Sainsbury's Blanc de Noirs
Champagne Brut   £21.00
Stalwart all-Pinot house champagne is still looking
smart behind its new gilded rococo label – on which
the Sainsbury's name is very discreet – and has elevated
modestly in price. Well-coloured wine with eager
mousse, brioche aromas and mellow lasting flavours;
12.5% alcohol. Top buy for this quality, and frequently
discounted. I have a magnum for which I paid £25.50 on
promo and intend to keep it a few years to see how it
turns out.

9 Taste the Difference Demi-Sec
Champagne   £18.00
'Demi-Sec' might summon up notions of sticky sweetness,
but well-made DS champagne is a greatly undervalued
treat. This one by elusive Epernay outfit Louis Kremer
(also producer of Morrisons house champagne) is really
only fractionally more 'sweet' than 'brut' wine and has a
wholesome mellowness all its own. If you don't like your
champagne too green, do try this; 12% alcohol.

Tesco

Just 30 wines this year from the market leader, but they're all good – and a good indicator too that Tesco still leads for quality as well as size when it comes to wine. Fifteen of my selection score 9 and five get the maximum. OK, I'll admit that I was the selector, by turning up at a couple of stores and buying wines I had every reason to hope would turn out for the best.

Usually, you see, I turn up at the jumbo Tesco tasting for the wine press, try a hundred or more wines and at leisure pick out the wines I believe to be worth recommending in these pages.

Standing in long queues in the midst of heatwaves or rainstorms – phenomena of the Summer of Covid already forgotten – in order to spend my limited budget on bottles of wine to deconstruct is a very much less convenient approach to this task. But I haven't had any choice. In lockdown I had to taste the wines alone, too, which didn't make the job any easier. And there were an awful lot of leftovers.

But enough about me. Tesco has come out of this process well. Its wines (and their prices) are holding steady and I am a happy customer.

RED WINES

ARGENTINA

🍷 8 **Tesco Argentinian Malbec 2019** £5.00
Party red of genuine ripeness and trim balance has juiciness and heft (13% alcohol); impressive value at this price.

🍷 8 **Trivento Malbec Private Reserve 2018** £10.00
I have long admired Argentina's Trivento brand, which has the benefit of ownership by Concha y Toro, maker of many of Chile's very best everyday wines. This is a deluxe item with textbook mulberry-leather Malbec aroma, darkly intense black fruits of beguiling minty-spicy sleekness, and a likeable cushiony plumpness; 14% alcohol. Not cheap, although I got mine at £8 on promo.

CHILE

🍷 8 **Finest Peumo Carmenère 2018** £9.00
Dark-chocolate-enrobed figs or prunes might come to the imaginative mind on sniffing and sipping this lushly oaked, crimson (carmine?) Colchagua wine. Even if it's just the nicely balanced black-cherry ripeness that inspires, this is a memorably satisfying red to drink with anything meaty; 13.5% alcohol.

FRANCE

🍷 9 **Tesco Beaujolais 2019** £5.00
Persistently likeable purple, bouncingly juicy and uplifting fun wine from a fine vintage for Beaujolais is a treat to drink straight from the fridge; 12.5% alcohol. This is the equal of any of its rivals and ridiculously cheap.

RED WINES

9   Réserve Des Tuguets Madiran 2017   £7.00

Tesco have been doing this Gascon wine since I was in short pants – mind you, I'm in short pants now, writing this amid the lockdown heat of summer 2020 – and I remember it being permanently discounted from a fanciful £10 or so to something nearer £6. Well, it's now listed at £7 (I paid £6 on promo) and it's been entirely worth it: beetroot colour, bright inky dense black-cherry fruit with spice and liquorice, a textbook Tannat with appropriate tannic grip and rugged charm; 13% alcohol.

8   Finest Malbec Cahors 2018   £7.50

The name Cahors – an ancient riverside town of the Lot Valley south of the Dordogne – was once known for its outstanding wines from the Malbec grape, but now it's the grape itself that takes precedence. I like this simple regional survivor for its spicy hedgerow charm and affable tannic grip; 13% alcohol.

8   Finest Faugères 2019   £9.00

I'm pleased Tesco are continuing with this rugged red from sun-scorched vineyards high above Beziers in the deep Languedoc. A genuine garrigue wine, wild with warm spiciness amid the juicy briar fruits with a modest 12.5% alcohol. Nice to drink young.

**10   Michel Chapoutier Côtes du
Rhône Villages 2018**   £9.00

Tesco reckon they're still listing this amazing ripe, succulent and elegantly spicy biodynamically made wine, awarded 10 in last year's edition, and no doubt an even better buy with more time in bottle; 14.5% alcohol. If the 2019 (another triumphant year in the Rhône) has superseded it, take a chance.

RED WINES

FRANCE

🍷 9 **Finest Montagne St Emilion 2018** £9.00
Opened this in a distracted moment to drink with Mexican black chilli beans and discovered that claret goes just fine with this sort of thing. In spite of its youth it was rounded and mellow and really rather ritzy, pitchy dark in colour with familiar cigar-box notes from oak and masses of intense mellow blackberry Merlot fruit, ripe (13.5% alcohol) and in elegant balance. I suppose it would have suited roast lamb better but black beans have never tasted better either.

🍷 10 **Ventoux Paul Jaboulet Aîné 2018** £10.00
Serendipity! Found this in the Wells Tesco reduced, needlessly, from £10 to £8. And it's gorgeous, a lovely maroon colour, scented with violets and garrigue, brilliant in its sunny spicy briar ripeness, generously hefty (14% alcohol) and beautifully trim at the finish.

ITALY

🍷 9 **Tesco Finest Montepulciano
d'Abruzzo 2018** £7.00
This has long been the best supermarket own-brand Montepulciano, this time showing plenty of bramble bounce and juicy freshness in its perky red fruits; 12.5% alcohol. Responds well to an hour or two in the fridge on summery occasions.

RED WINES

ITALY

♟ 9 Finest Valpolicella Ripasso 2017 £11.00

In spite of a 'challenging' vintage in 2017 this has turned out to be a particularly velvety and brightly juicy wine from top Verona co-op Cantina Valpantena, a benchmark for the darkly enriched ripasso style; 13.5% alcohol. I would certainly take the 2018 on trust.

PORTUGAL

♟ 10 Tesco Douro 2017 £6.00

The price has crept up forgivably modestly from last year's £5.75 but the 2017, still listed at deadline, has lost none of its miraculous charm: dark beetroot colour, keen minty black fruit, warmly spicy tannin, good heft (13.5% alcohol) and of course still-incomprehensible price. If you find the 2018, don't hesitate.

SPAIN

♟ 8 Tesco Viña del Cura Rioja Crianza 2017 £6.75

Not granted 'Finest' designation like its Reserva stablemate this is nevertheless a decently ripe and complete crianza with a proper vanilla lick and clear cassis fruit; 13.5% alcohol.

♟ 9 Pulpito Toro Tempranillo 2017 £8.00

I liked this quite a lot last year – 'pleasingly abrasive and ripe … hallmark black-pepper savours and substance' and I like it even better now, because the price has plummeted from £11 to £8. Oddly but eyecatchingly labelled with an illustration of an octopus (*pulpito* in Spanish) it's generous and delicious; 13.5% alcohol.

RED WINES

SPAIN

 9 **Finest Viña del Cura Rioja Reserva 2015** £8.50

Nice slickness to this new vintage is no doubt largely down to the vanilla creaminess of oak contact, but the well-defined cassis-raspberry fruit has a sleek juiciness of its own, and the balance is very pleasing; 13.5% alcohol. Made by big but dedicated bodega Baron de Ley.

WHITE WINES

AUSTRALIA

8 **Finest Tingleup Riesling 2019** £9.00

Howard Park in Denmark (that's Denmark in Western Australia) produces this intriguing limey (in the citrus sense) wine in a style very different from the German method with Riesling; it's dry and assertive in its crunchy red-apple fruit, tangy and long with 12.5% alcohol. If you like Aussie Riesling, you should really like this; if you're new to it, this is a nifty introduction.

FRANCE

9 **Finest Côtes de Gascogne Blanc 2019** £6.50

Lovely limey-floral racy dry refresher artfully concocted from Colombard and Gros Manseng grapes by Gascony's brilliant Plaimont Producteurs; 11.5% alcohol. Anytime wine at a very keen price.

9 **Finest St Mont 2018** £6.50

Fine gold colour and intriguing sun-baked landscape aromas of orchard blossom and meadow herb lead into a basket of fruit flavours embracing apple and peach, melon and mango. Made by Plaimont in Gascony, it's a dry wine but complex and full of summer ripeness; 13.5% alcohol.

WHITE WINES

FRANCE

🍷 9   **Finest Picpoul de Pinet 2019**   **£7.50**
Full-bottomed rendition of this fashionable and characterful Mediterranean seafood-matcher has greeny-gold colour and tangy, saline heft, and yet it's keenly refreshing and uplifting; 13% alcohol. Smart package and good price.

🍷 8   **Finest Sancerre 2019**   **£14.00**
You're paying for the name of the Loire Valley's most vaunted Sauvignon appellation, but this wine does stand out from the crowd: glinting pale gold colour, big waft of river-fresh, pebbly minerality, lush nettly classic fruit flavours, long and elegantly limey in its finish; 13% alcohol.

ITALY

🍷 8   **Finest Passerina 2019**   **£7.00**
Attractive ornithological label references the tale that this Abruzzo wine's constituent Passerina grape is named after a sparrow-like species of bird that feeds off the vines. It's certainly an attractive wine: warm sunny colour, ripe orchard and stone fruit flavours, mineral but lush, briskly dry and tangy; 13% alcohol.

🍷 8   **Finest Pecorino 2018**   **£7.00**
Grassy and lush in keeping with the (partly imaginary) pasture country of the Abruzzo in Italy's east midlands where the Pecorino grape prospers, this is somehow a thoroughly Italian dry white – tangy but long, mineral but plump with crisp white fruits; 13% alcohol.

🍷 9   **Finest Beneventano Greco 2017**   **£9.00**
Autumn colour and flavours come through in this maturing Campania dry wine, lifted by a lively citrus acidity; 13% alcohol. Do try it for its complex herbaceous and hot-house-fruits nuances, adaptable to tricky menus as well as a contemplative aperitif.

WHITE WINES

SOUTH AFRICA

🍷 8 **Finest Fairtrade South African Chenin Blanc 2019** £7.50

Almost austere by Cape Chenin Blanc standards, this nevertheless has an alluring honeysuckle nose, leading into zingy orchard-fruit flavours with a very lively citrus acidity; 12.5% alcohol. Note the Fairtrade designation – it means a lot.

SPAIN

🍷 9 **Finest Viñas del Rey Albariño 2019** £8.50

Big saline flavours in this generous, greenly-lush dry wine from Rias Baixas on Spain's wild Atlantic coast; 12.5% alcohol. The vines are trained high above ground on stately pergolas to maximise the cooling effect of ocean breezes during the hot ripening season, and the briny allusion is easily imaginable when you taste the wine.

FORTIFIED WINES

PORTUGAL

🍷 9 **Finest 10-Year-Old-Tawny Port** £12.50

Aged-in-cask tawny is the best kind of port. It is the silkiest of after-dinner sips, but at home in Portugal majors as an aperitif, chilled straight from the fridge. This one, more affordable than the big-name brands but made by the Symington family, owners of several of the big brands, has a fine copper colour, enticing figgy-sweet-nut perfume and silky, deliciously fiery fruit; 20% alcohol.

FORTIFIED WINES

9 Finest Fino Sherry 37.5cl £6.00
Only in stores with the widest wine ranges, this is worth
seeking out: a bone-dry pale sherry of star quality made by
Gonzalez Byass of Tio Pepe fame and, um, not dissimilar
in style – or price. Arguably the greatest aperitif wine of
them all, under the Tesco name, with 15% alcohol and
one condition: serve very cold.

SPARKLING WINES

8 Finest 1531 Blanquette de Limoux £9.00
It's a vintage wine, but 2016 rather than 1531. The earlier
date is reportedly the year in which monks at Limoux's
Saint-Hilaire priory discovered what we now call the
champagne method of making sparkling wine – 150 years
before other monks in the Champagne region did so.
Blanquette is the original grape, now under another name,
Mauzac. (It's a parallel in nomenclature to Prosecco, the
name of the grape in the notorious Italian wine, now
restyled Glera, reserving the name for the fizz itself.)
Anyway, this is an excellent Blanquette, fully sparkling,
crisp and orchardy, fresh and friendly, not too dry and
12.5% alcohol. Same price area as prosecco – 500 times
better.

10 Finest Premier Cru Champagne Brut £20.00
Always generous in colour and in yeasty-bakery aromas,
this thrilling sparkler, from *grand cru* as well as *premier
cru* vineyards, really does taste a cut above a 'supermarket
champagne'. I could list several brands, vastly more
expensive, that don't come close. Quality – at a rational
price; 12.5% alcohol.

SPARKLING WINES

FRANCE

🏆 10 Finest Vintage Grand Cru Blanc de
Blanc Champagne Brut 2012 £26.00

Richly coloured and mellow, yet full of bright flavours
and freshness, this lavish pure Chardonnay champagne
from top-rated (*Grand Cru*) vineyards in a seriously
good vintage year is nicely packaged and worthy of any
celebration; 12.5% alcohol. It is a wonder to me there is
still any left, at what is a very modest price for this sort of
thing.

SPAIN

🍷 9 Tesco Cava Brut £5.75

Catalonia's traditional sparkling wine cava has been all but
washed out of the market by the torrent of prosecco. The
injustice is amply illustrated by this bargain true sparkler:
eager, lively, full of crisp orchard fruit and notably just
11.5% alcohol (the same as prosecco). And of course it's
far cheaper than even the dullest manifestations of its
Venetian rival.

Waitrose

 The queues at Waitrose (& Partners) have been decorous. My nearest store, in Gillingham, Dorset, happens to have a covered walkway extending along two sides of the building. Under its roof shoppers can shelter from searing sunlight or tempestuous downpours in calm comfort.

I have joined these patient lines several times over the viral months and while social distancing has ensured near-monastic silences between participants, a well-intentioned resignation, a slyly humorous solidarity of apathy, has prevailed and has helped ease the anxiety.

The wines have been well worth the trouble and expense, and I commend the 60-or-so red, white, pink, fortified and fizzy items described in the following pages.

Waitrose has, I hope, weathered the year well. We all know, or think we know, that the supermarkets benefited from the closure of restaurants, pubs and so on, but even before the virus struck, Waitrose's owner John Lewis (& Partners) had announced plummeting profits, and that planned 2020 store closures would include Waitrose branches. From about now (September 2020) Waitrose loses its Ocado-supplier role to M&S, which won't help.

For all that, Waitrose's wine offering has been easily the most robust in terms of range, innovation and price promotion through the year. Waitrose's store count (about 340) is less than half of Aldi's or Lidl's, let alone the Big Four chains, but its wine list (more than 1,000 items) is vastly more numerous and diverse than any of theirs.

Waitrose wine, frankly, is a unique phenomenon in UK retailing. Junk brands are largely eschewed, just about every producing region of the world is represented, serious celebration wines are there for those who aspire to them, and prices are not only fair but perpetually discounted, often substantially. Waitrose carried on with its regular wine promotions throughout the Covid crisis, and for the first week of July 2020, coinciding with the reopening of pubs, bars and restaurants, staged a bumper promotion: 25 per cent off every wine in the range.

Waitrose is here to stay.

RED WINES

ARGENTINA

🍷 8 **Beefsteak Club Malbec 2019**   £8.99
In spite of the naff packaging, I was quite taken with this muscular but friendly wine, darkly savoury in the Mendoza way with Malbec, spicily centred and not overweight; 13.5% alcohol. No doubt fine with beef, maybe burger rather than baron.

🍷 8 **Norton Coleccion Malbec 2019**   £10.49
Smooth darkly roasty-savoury typical Mendoza Malbec summons notions of rich blackberry pie; artfully weighted and very easy to like, especially at occasional promo price of £6.99; 14% alcohol.

CHILE

🍷 8 **Waitrose Blueprint Reserva Chilean
Carmenère 2017**   £7.49
I do get what Waitrose say about 'hints of tobacco on the nose' of this fine wine. It's a kind of benevolent pungency rather than anything sinister, and adds to the spicy-sweet appeal of the dark cassis flavours in this mature Rapel pure varietal; 14% alcohol.

FRANCE

🍷 10 **Cuvée Chasseur 2019**   £5.49
I hunted high and low for this constant friend and finally found a bottle – and it's brilliant. Mediterranean-made from a curious mix of Merlot with Grenache among others it's a wholesome evocation of generously sun-ripened hedgerow fruits; 12% alcohol. Well done Waitrose for holding the price.

RED WINES

Waitrose

FRANCE

8 **Cuvée des Vigneronnes Beaujolais** £7.79
Dependable non-vintage wine made by giant producer
Duboeuf is rather expensive (although I got mine on promo
at £6.29) but juicy and ripe; 12.5% alcohol.

9 **L'Arène des Anges Costières
de Nîmes 2018** £7.99
Named for the city of Nîmes' superbly preserved Roman
arena, a bold and spicy Grenache–Syrah blend in the best
briary southern Rhône tradition with the extra sunburnt
twang that characterises this appellation; 14% alcohol.
Good price, and I've seen it on promo at just £5.99.

8 **Malbec de Balthazar Pays d'Oc 2018** £8.69
Still on shelf from last year is this perky middleweight
wine in spite of Malbec's good name for heft, and has
a juicy sun-kissed blackberry charm on nose and palate;
12.5% alcohol. It's been on promo at a keen £6.49.

9 **Remy Ferbras Ventoux 2018** £8.99
Right on cue, a cracking new vintage of this rollicking
Rhône red from the vineyards of Mont Ventoux, a cone-
shaped demi-mountain notorious as one of the toughest
climbs along the route of the Tour de France. Ferbras
slipped up in 2017, I thought, but this year is back in
the saddle with an intensely dark, spicy and lingeringly
savoury wine; 13% alcohol. Regularly discounted to
£6.99.

RED WINES

FRANCE

10 Les Nivières Saumur 2017   **£9.99**
Maturing Loire Cabernet Franc has a rush of purple red
fruit of utterly delicious and distinctive character; 12.5%
alcohol. Great match for saucy fish dishes, cured meats
and all sorts of poultry and game. Chills well for enjoying
on long, hot summer days. Do try this Waitrose-exclusive
wine – I fear that Loire reds (Saumur, Chinon and
Bourgueil) face supermarket extinction and this would be
a great loss.

**8 Réserve des Hospitaliers Côtes du
      Rhône Villages 2018**   **£11.99**
Part of the blend for this muscular wine is reportedly
aged awhile in new oak casks. It does have an appreciable
silkiness along with its sinew and it's fair for Waitrose to
say it "gives Châteauneuf a run for its money". Darkly
spicy intensely ripe fruit; 14% alcohol.

9 Guigal Côtes du Rhône 2016   **£12.79**
I am warming to this successor to the fabled 2015 vintage
as bottle-age mellows the intense spicy fruit into silky
luscious ripeness; 13.5% alcohol. Clearly a wine that
will develop for years yet: it may be just ordinary Côtes
du Rhône AC, but this is one of the great wines of that
appellation, and 2016 is reckoned a five-star vintage. This
wine is occasionally offered on promo at £9.99 – a real
deal, snap it up if you see it.

RED WINES

FRANCE

🍷 **8** **Cave de St Désirat Saint Joseph 2018** £15.99

St Joseph is a northern Rhône appellation for pure-Syrah reds that can come close in quality to fabulously expensive neighbouring ACs Côte Rôtie and Hermitage. This one has a rich crimson colour, fine ripe raspberry perfume and big blackberry fruit with sun-baked spice and a good grip of friendly tannin; 13.5% alcohol. This has been discounted to £12.79 on occasion and would repay keeping a year or three.

🍷 **8** **Joseph Drouhin Rully 2017** £19.99

Up in price from last year's spiffy 2015 vintage (£16.99), this is still a very tempting buy – limpid and seductive with raspberry-violet perfume and earthy-sweet classic Chalonnais Pinot fruit; 13% alcohol.

GREECE

🍷 **9** **Tsantali Organic Cabernet Sauvignon 2017** £9.99

Old favourite with a jazzy new label – I nearly missed it on the shelf – has a bright blackcurranty bloom and sleek but perky matching fruit, all in fine even elegant balance; 13% alcohol. The style owes something to the modern Bordeaux method, but this is from northern Greece's coastal resort region of Halkidiki, and knowing that somehow adds something to its overall appeal.

RED WINES

ITALY

⚱ 9   Recchia Bardolino 2019   **£8.79**

The diaphanous delights of Verona's delicate red deserve to come back into fashion if reds like this become the benchmark. It's a scintillating cherry-bright refresher with fleeting fruit sweetness perkily balanced by the crisp nutskin-dry finish; a fine aperitif to serve cool and a good match for an Italian feast, especially one including antipasto and cured meats like Parma ham and salami; 12.5% alcohol.

⚱ 9   Borgodei Trulli Salice Salentino 2018   **£8.99**

Persistently delectable dark, rich and savoury Puglian wine from evocatively named Negroamaro grapes is particularly ripe and full in this vintage (13.5% alcohol); obligingly pruny, earthy and even suggesting bitter chocolate. Waitrose regularly offers this wine on discount at £6.99, which is a steal.

⚱ 8   Triade Rosso 2017   **£8.99**

The Puglian trio are local grape varieties – from the south eastern Adriatic coast of Italy – Negroamaro, Primitivo and Nero di Troia, cohering into a deep crimson colour, spiky blackberry nose and savoury-spicy-toasty briar fruit with easy tannin providing a finishing style ideally suited to matching sticky pasta dishes; 13.5% alcohol. Regularly on promo at £6.74.

RED WINES

ITALY

10 **Terre di Faiano Primitivo 2019**   £9.99

I first bought this wine after believing I'd seen a bottle in an episode of *Montalbano*. But it turned out to be from the mainland region of Puglia rather than the TV detective's native Sicily, so perhaps I'm not on the right case. Never mind, this is a real discovery. It's organically made, soupily dense and plump, savoury and gently spicy and as distinctive as its orange livery suggests; 13.5% alcohol. Perpetually on promo at a bargain £7.49.

8 **Cecchi Morellino di Scansano 2018**   £9.99

Sweet but neat Tuscan wine from Maremma is largely from the Sangiovese grape of Chianti renown but here makes a more delicate cherry-ripe style that manages to convey good weight and balance with a little sprinkle of white pepper; 13% alcohol.

8 **Montidori Sangiovese 2018**   £9.99

I'm not sure the dark dumpy bottle is much of a lure, but this Chianti-grape wine from Emilia-Romagna (not really a wine region unless you count Lambrusco) is a suitably dark and dense confection made by the ever-multiplying ripasso method (which kicked off with Valpolicella in the Veneto); 13% alcohol. Up in price from last year but occasionally discounted. Waitrose suggest it will make a good accompaniment to spaghetti bolognese or a rich ragu, and I'm inclined to agree.

RED WINES

ITALY

🍷 **8** **Terre di Faiano Nero d'Avola**
Appassimento 2019 **£9.99**
Couldn't wait to try this new stablemate to the
fabled Primitivo on page 136. It's a darkly promising
varietal of Sicily from the island's native grape Nero
d'Avola (Avola being a wee town in the island's
southeast), organically produced and reinforced by
the appassimento method (see glossary). It's good,
balancing sweetly black-cherry-ripe fruit with a keen,
drying acidity and thoroughly healthy; 13.5% alcohol.

🍷 **9** **Paolo Leo Primitivo di Manduria 2018** **£10.99**
Still on shelf from last year this big cushiony Salento
wine evokes plums, cinnamon and sweet black cherries
in its roasty-savoury dark flavours; trim finish and 14%
alcohol.

🍷 **9** **Masi Campofiorin Verona Rosso 2016** **£12.99**
Still on sale a year later in the fine vintage of 2016, this
unique perennial favourite is presumably not selling in
spite of regular discounts to £9.99. It has materially
mellowed since I last tasted it, readily confirming its
keeping qualities (up to 20 years, says Masi), showing
cushiony-plump black-cherry flavours with notions of
plum, cinnamon, violets and marzipan. Hefty in the
amarone style with a tannic cut it's nevertheless very easy
drinking and a modest 13% alcohol.

RED WINES

ITALY

8 **Waitrose Valpolicella Classico Ripasso**
Superiore Fratelli Recchia 2017 £13.99
A mouthful not just in nomenclature, this is substantially
forthcoming in flavour terms too: ripe black-cherry fruit
is firmed up with gently abrasive bitter-chocolate/coffee
notes finishing dry to make a deluxe match for roast lamb
or beef as well as pongy cheeses; 14.5% alcohol. Not
cheap, but notably well made.

9 **Terre del Barolo 2015** £19.99
I bought a bottle of this on promo after liking it at the
2019 tasting and opened it in summer 2020 to find it
had developed a nice little bit of orange hue, a gamey
pong and silky slickness of texture to the spicy-smoky red
fruits; really interesting wine, described grandiloquently
by Waitrose as 'imperious, powerful, elegant'; 14%
alcohol.

PORTUGAL

9 **Gran Passo Classico Tinto 2017** £7.99
New vintage for this quirky generic wine from grapes
including Tinta Franca (Port country) and Syrah
(southern France) from a winemaker who, in the words
of Waitrose wine buyer Nick Room 'obviously likes
motor scooters'. The clue's on the label. And this is a
screwcap wine – from the nation that makes corks. The
wine is inkily dark and savoury in the proper Portuguese
minty-clovey style with vanilla richness and a firm grip
on the tastebuds to boot; 14% alcohol. Good price, and
it's been on promo at just £6.49.

RED WINES

10 Waitrose Douro Reserva 2017 £11.49

This is made for Waitrose by Quinta de la Rosa, a family Port estate that diversified in the 1990s into making table wines (red and white) and has led the way for inspired quality ever since. This fabulous wine has dense maroon colour, seductive pruny-minty-porty nose and silky developed black-fruit flavours; 14% alcohol. Already drinking beautifully in spite of its youth, it's easily the best Douro red I can remember from any year – and so especially welcome in these distraught times. Quinta de la Rosa is a family enterprise with steeply terraced vines running down to the river in the Cima Corgo near the valley's little railway town of Pinhao.

PORTUGAL

9 Castillo de Olite Navarra Tinto 2013 £9.49

There appears to be an inexhaustible supply of this nicely developed earthy sweetly oaked Tempranillo–Garnacha blend from the underrated Navarra region, still manifested in the 2013 vintage as it was here last year but now £9.49, down from £9.99, and regularly discounted to £7.49. Aged 18 months in oak before bottling, it's warming and wholesome and 13.5% alcohol.

SPAIN

RED WINES

🍷 10 The Cubist Garnacha 2017 £9.99

From gnarly old vines planted in 'extremely poor soil' (Waitrose's own words) in the arid, hermetic Catalayud region south of Rioja, this wine has been a perennial at Waitrose since the year dot but only under the fancy assumed name The Cubist since about 2012. The 2017 is fantastically good, bursting with bright red fruits of bracing, sinewy, spicy vitality, very intense and ripe and with 14.5% alcohol. It even has a fancy stopper, 'the world's first zero carbon footprint wine closure' from 'renewable plant-based materials derived from sugar cane'. The 2018 is expected soon, I gather. Invest with confidence.

🍷 9 Torres Celeste Ribera del Duero 2016 £12.99

Really attractively packaged (suitably, celestially starry) special-occasion red from the Ribera del Duero outpost of Catalan producer Torres. It's barrel-fermented pure Tempranillo in the lush eucalyptus Ribera style of intense creamy black-fruit savour, mellow in its maturity; 14.5% alcohol. I got mine at £9.99 on promo.

SPAIN

Waitrose

RED WINES

 USA

8 **Drouhin Dundee Hills Pinot**
Noir 2015 £36.49
Well, you wouldn't expect it to fly off the shelves, so I
feel safe reprising this from last year's edition for which
I very much enjoyed tasting it. You get a lovely silky
Oregon Pinot very much in the Burgundy tradition
(Drouhin is a star in the region) plush with ripeness and
14% alcohol.

PINK WINES

 FRANCE

8 Jardin de Roses 2019 £13.49
Slightly self-conscious bottling – fancy shape, rose-garden
botanical illustration (there's a whole series, I believe) – of
a very decent Languedoc pink by ubiquitous Jean-Claude
Mas is pale but decidely interesting with crisp red fruits,
tangy citrus lift and palpable freshness; 12.5% alcohol.
Got this on promo at very fair £9.99.

 ITALY

8 **Borgodei Trulli Primitivo**
Rosato 2019 £8.99
From the producer of the excellent Salice Salentino (see
page 135) comes this firmly flavoured red-summer-
fruit citrus twangy dry and impressively refreshing al
fresco pink from the highly desirable Primitive grape;
12.5% alcohol. Waitrose boast it makes the perfect
accompaniment to any occasion – let's put that to the test.

PINK WINES

ITALY

🍷 8 **La Carezza Pinot Nero 2019** £10.99
Delicate pale colour belies the assertive, crisply defined
Pinot Noir flavours in this Venetian dry wine, a convincing
rendition of the grape's cherry-strawberry fruitiness and
tight balancing acidity; 12% alcohol. Not cheap – but I
got mine at £7.99 on promo.

WHITE WINES

AUSTRIA

🍷 8 **Waitrose Blueprint Grüner
Veltliner 2019** £7.99
Aromatic and pleasingly integrating elements of white
peach and white pepper in the easy heft of its rather lush
orchardy fruit, this is a standout wine fully deserving
its growing popularity, especially as an aperitif and a
matching for Asian flavours; 12.5% alcohol.

FRANCE

🍷 9 **Cuvée Pêcheur 2019** £5.49
Perpetual top buy from Gascony made from big-cropping
Ugni Blanc and Colombard grapes, mostly grown for
production of Armagnac brandy, but here producing
a masterly dry white bright with meadow scents and
aromatic fruits; fresh fun and consistent both in quality
and value; 11.5% alcohol.

🍷 8 **Sous le Soleil du Midi
Chardonnay 2019** £5.99
Nice contrivance made in the south of the country from
grapes 'from different parts of France'. It's Chardonnay
in the crisp red-apple style with perhaps a little coconut
oak in the mix and a genuinely sunny ripeness; 13%
alcohol. Nice package, charming wine.

WHITE WINES

FRANCE

🍷 8 Le Grand Ballon Sauvignon Blanc 2019 £8.99

Touraine (Loire Valley) wine of hazy provenance is river-fresh with lively grassy-nettly green flavours in the approved Sauvignon tradition. It also scores for leesy intensity and a long, limey finish; 12% alcohol. The price does not appear inflated for the quality of the wine, which is always a bonus.

🍷 8 Côtes du Rhône Blanc Gabriel Meffre 2019 £9.99

Fine mélange of fruits in this dry but full and ripe blend of Grenache Blanc with Viognier and Roussanne: apple and lime – quite a range of fruit flavours, you'll agree, but all individually discernible. 13% alcohol. Has been on promo at £7.49.

🍷 9 Alsace Gewürztraminer Paul Blanck 2018 £14.99

The trouble with supermarket generic Alsace Gewürzes is that most of them are made by the same giant co-op (at Türckheim if you need to know) which means that they all taste the same and they're too sweet. OK they generally cost under a tenner, but I don't think they're worth it. Now here's one by a splendid (if large-scale) individual grower at Kientzheim that fully warrants the extra premium. It's richly coloured, blooming with lychee and roses, exotically spicy and lush in the approved manner and in fine balance, grapy rather than sweet; 13.5% alcohol.

WHITE WINES

🍷 **8** **Sancerre Domaine Naudet 2019** £14.99

Waitrose's exclusive Sancerre – Naudet has only 30 acres of Sauvignon – is ripe and intense (13.5% alcohol) in this vintage, big with the classic Sauvignon notes of asparagus and grassy lushness in its pebble-fresh, citrus-lifted leesy flavours.

🍷 **8** **Domaine Masson-Blondelet**
Pouilly-Fumé 2019 £15.99

Now we have an irresistible opportunity to juxtapose two similarly named but entirely distinct wines. Pouilly-sur-Loire is a quintessential French riverside town not far from Sancerre in the central Loire Valley. The dry white wines it makes, from Sauvignon Blanc grapes, are called Pouilly-Fumé and compare favourably with Sancerre. This one has fine fruit-blossom and raspberry aromas, glittering grassy-nettly fruit and river-pebble-like freshness; 12.5% alcohol. The Pouilly-Fuissé immediately below is another thing altogether.

🍷 **9** **Marc Dudet Pouilly-Fuissé 2019** £17.99

The Mâconnais in southern Burgundy does Chardonnay in its own way and Pouilly-Fuissé does its Mâconnais in its own further-refined way. This young wine tells the story, its glorious minerality referencing Pouilly's distinct clay soil over the universal limestone of the region, its richness of sweet-apple fruit (13% alcohol) clearly a signature. Well, that's the way I see it. A revelatory wine already thrilling, and probably capable of development. But when a wine is as ready and appetizing as this, who would wait?

WHITE WINES

**8 Saint-Aubin Premier Cru Domaine
Gérard Thomas 2018   £25.99**

Look, I haven't tasted this. But last year I tasted the
2016 ('lemon-gold ... floral fleetingly nectareous oaked
Chardonnay aromas ... leesy lush fruit') and fully
expect that this will be comparable; the price, believe it
or not, is quite reasonable for this kind of thing. Worth
splashing out on a special occasion.

**8 Waitrose Blueprint Dry German
Riesling 2019   £7.99**

This one comes recommended, I gather, by TV presenter
Philip Schofield, it's a breezy moselle with good colour,
green-apple crispness and a finishing tang, dry and racy;
12% alcohol. Waitrose suggest pairing it with smoked
meats or chilled as an aperitif. Is Schofield, I wonder, a
name of German origin?

9 Dr L Grey Slate Riesling 2018   £5.99

You don't need to be a geologist to get the ground-
conditions connections with the style of this wine: it has
minerality at the core of its flavour and texture. Ponder
that! The zingy fruit has typical Riesling crisp-apple
crunch but there's a lush lick of peachiness here too. An
ingenious contrivance from unfailingly innovative Dr
Loosen; 10.5% alcohol.

WHITE WINES

🍷 **8** **Georg Mosbacher Deidesheimer**
Herrgottsacker Riesling Trocken 2018   £14.99
Modern dry fermented-out (12.5% alcohol) Rheinpfalz
estate wine; minerally and elegant with plenty of crisp
green-apple Riesling fruit and a friendly lick of sweeter-
apple ripeness too. This is food wine: fish or shellfish,
cured meats and so on.

🍷 **9** **Dr Loosen Urziger Würzgarten**
Riesling Kabinett 2019   £15.99
Zippy new vintage of this ravishing Moselle is
preternaturally pure and racing in its mineral-malic
sublime Riesling fruit; Waitrose call it 'light-bodied'
but it seems to me powerfully intense and impactful
as well as thrillingly refreshing and enlivening; 8%
alcohol.

🍷 **9** **Willi Haag Brauneberger Juffer**
Sonnenuhr Riesling Auslese 2018   £19.99
To my mortification, the 2016 vintage of this wine,
praised to the skies in the last edition, has sold out. I
know they've got the 2018 vintage (in six giant stores or
online only) but haven't tasted it. Just for reference here's
what I said about the 2016: 'The colour is rich gold, the
perfume honeyed but edgy with citrus, the fruit gloriously
autumnal with suggestions of botrytis but racy, lemon-
limey fresh and defined. It's rare to find a world-class
wine like this in a supermarket and only six Waitrose
branches stock it but you can buy it online at Waitrose
Cellar. Price is entirely warranted.'

WHITE WINES

8 Pecorino Terre di Chieti 2019 £7.99
Cheery sheep decorate the fun label of this Abruzzo dry
white because it is believed that the grape name Pecorino
is a diminutive of the Italian *pecaro* meaning sheep. The
wine is crisp and dry but admittedly grassy, and pleasingly
fresh in its nutty, grapefruity Italian way; 13% alcohol.

**8 Waitrose Blueprint Soave
Classico 2019** £7.99
Dumpy looking bottle but really lively style to this
full-flavoured rendering of the classic Verona dry
white: whiffs of blossom and brassica, keen mineral
freshness to the apple-nectarine fruit with hallmark
blanched-almond suggestion and trim citrus edge;
12.5% alcohol.

9 Zenato Villa Flora Lugana 2019 £11.99
This wine is a Waitrose exclusive, and has been made
specially from Trebbiano grapes by the Zenato winery
in the little DOC of Lugana south of Lake Garda for 25
years. Happy anniversary! This new vintage has a fine
floral bloom, combines flinty freshness with ripe peach,
melon and white nut lushness and emerges in uplifting
tangy acidity; 13% alcohol. Occasionally on promo at
£9.49 – a major bargain. Waitrose recommend it with
white meats, shellfish or pasta.

WHITE WINES

NEW ZEALAND

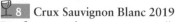

🍷 8 **Waitrose Blueprint New Zealand Sauvignon Blanc 2019** £7.99

Sensibly priced Marlborough wine with authentic Kiwi glitter of grassy-nettly fruit, gooseberry aromas and tangy citrus acidity; 12.5% alcohol.

🍷 8 **Crux Sauvignon Blanc 2019** £10.49

Big flavours of asparagus as well as tropical fruits and a clear grapefruit twang in this assertive Marlborough wine; 12.5% alcohol. Good competitive food matcher, and I've seen it on promo at a third off – £6.99.

SPAIN

🍷 8 **Palacio de Fefiñanes Albariño 2019** £15.99

The last word from Rias Baixas? The breezy-briny Albariños of Galicia's Atlantic-facing gastronomic paradise deserve their popularity. This is a deluxe spin on the theme: bold white orchard fruits with seagrass raciness and limey twang, a memorable match for fishy dishes, even the most emphatically flavoured; 13% alcohol.

FORTIFIED WINES

PORTUGAL

🍷 9 **Sandeman 20-Year-Old Tawny Port** £39.99

As long as Waitrose stocks this rare and wonderful wine, I will mention it here. As reported previously, it's a sublime copper colour, creamily fiery in its pure fruit flavours, silky, rich and balanced; 20% alcohol. Regular promos reducing the price to £31.99 continue.

FORTIFIED WINES

**10 Waitrose Blueprint Amontillado
Sherry** £7.69

Definingly good house sherry is billed as Medium Dry, which might have indicated some sort of chicanery, as Amontillado is, strictly speaking, dry. But this is not confection, it's perfection: gorgeous mahogany colour, thrilling pungent sweet-nut and fig compote nose, keen toasty-smoky flavours, endlessly nuanced; 18.5% alcohol. Drink chilled as an aperitif or any temperature with after dinner treats.

**9 Waitrose Blueprint Manzanilla
Fino Sherry** £7.69

Manzanilla is the pale, dry sherry of the coastal town of Sanlucar de Barrameda in Andalusia. It's the seaside counterpart and rival of Fino, the pale, dry sherry of Jerez de la Frontera, in the Andalusian interior. You could spend a lifetime comparing the merits of the two styles. The principal distinction, I suppose, is that Manzanilla, made and matured in bodegas very close to the sea, is supposed to absorb a certain salty tang as it ages. In landlocked Jerez, the air isn't the same. See if you get the briny brio in this lovely bone-dry, very pale example; 15% alcohol. Serve very cold.

SPARKLING WINES

🍷 9 **Cave de Lugny Crémant de Bourgogne**
Blanc de Blancs £13.99
A marvellously consistent sparkler from one of the
leading co-operatives of the Mâconnais in Burgundy's
southern reaches, this all-Chardonnay wine lives up
to its description *crémant* both in the flow of its tiny-
bubble mousse and the mellowness of its rich sweet-
apple fruit; 12% alcohol. Another consistency here
is the almost perpetual promotional price of £10.49
– and that makes this a rare bargain.

🍷 9 **Waitrose Blanc de Noirs**
Champagne Brut £23.99
This is all from Pinot Noir grapes, reportedly mostly
from the 2015 harvest but with the addition of older
reserve wines, making for what I now see I referred
to last year as 'movingly mellow and calming'. I don't
know whether to laugh or cry at this diversion from the
objective, but promise I still like this champagne very
much, especially when it's on offer at 20 per cent off,
which it often is; 12% alcohol.

🍷 8 **Waitrose Blanc de Blancs**
Champagne Brut £23.99
Pure Chardonnay wine and it shows in the creamy-
yeasty orchardy perfume and decidedly mature
corresponding flavours. I have no idea why it's priced
higher than its companion Blanc de Noirs (above);
12.5% alcohol.

SPARKLING WINES

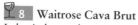

8 Waitrose Cava Brut   £9.99

I don't know how many proseccos Waitrose sells but
I've tasted a few of them over the years, and remain
convinced that this Catalan contender knocks the
lot of them firmly into a cocked hat. This is a fully
fizzy, champagne-method (well, traditional method
as the litigious champenois would insist on calling it)
abounding in delightful white-fruit refreshing flavours;
11.5% alcohol.

Enjoying it

Drink or keep?

Wines from supermarkets should be ready to drink as soon as you get them home. Expensive reds of recent vintage, for example from Bordeaux or the Rhône, sold as seasonal specials, might benefit from a few years' 'cellaring'. If in doubt, look up your purchase on a web vintage chart to check.

Some wines certainly need drinking sooner than others. Dry whites and rosés won't improve with time. Good-quality red wines will happily endure, even improve, for years if they're kept at a constant moderate temperature, preferably away from bright light, and on their sides so corks don't dry out. Supermarkets like to advise us on back labels of red wines to consume the product within a year or two. Pay no attention.

Champagne, including supermarket own-label brands, almost invariably improves with keeping. Evolving at rest is what champagne is all about. Continue the process at home. I like to wait for price promotions, buy in bulk and hoard the booty in smug certainty of a bargain that's also an improving asset. None of this applies to any other kind of sparkling wine – especially prosecco.

Of more immediate urgency is the matter of keeping wine in good condition once you've opened it. Recorked leftovers should last a day, but after that the wine will oxidise, turning stale and sour. There is a variety of wine-saving stopper devices, but I have yet to find one that works. My preferred method is to decant leftovers into a smaller bottle with a pull-cork or screwcap. Top it right up.

Early opening

Is there any point in uncorking a wine in advance to allow it to 'breathe'? Absolutely none. The stale air trapped between the top of the wine and the bottom of the cork (or screwcap) disperses at once and the 1cm circle of liquid exposed will have a negligible response to the atmosphere. Decanting the wine will certainly make a difference, but whether it's a beneficial difference is a matter for conjecture – unless you're decanting to get the wine off its lees or sediment.

Beware trying to warm up an icy bottle of red. If you put it close to a heat source, take the cork out first. As the wine warms, even mildly, it gives off gas that will spoil the flavour if it cannot escape.

Chill factor

White wine, rosé and sparkling wines all need to be cold. It's the law. The degree of chill is a personal choice but icy temperatures can mask the flavours of good wines. Bad wines, on the other hand, might benefit from overchilling. The anaesthetic effect removes the sense of taste.

Red wines can respond well to mild chilling. Beaujolais and stalky reds of the Loire such as Chinon and Saumur are brighter when cool, as is Bardolino from Verona and lighter Pinot Noir from everywhere.

Is it off?

Once there was a plague of 'corked' wine. It's over. Wine bottlers have eliminated most of the causes. Principal among them was TCA or trichloroanisole 123, an infection of the raw material from which corks are made, namely the bark of cork oak trees. New technology developed by firms such as Portuguese cork giant Amorim has finally made all cork taint-free.

TCA spawned an alternative-closure industry that has prospered mightily through the supply of polymer stoppers and screwcaps. The polymer products, although unnecessary now that corks are so reliable, persist. They're pointless: awkward to extract and to reinsert, and allegedly less environmentally friendly than natural corks.

Screwcaps persist too, but they have their merits. They obviate the corkscrew and can be replaced on the bottle. They are recyclable. Keep them on the bottles you take to the bottle bank.

Some closures will, of course, occasionally fail due to material faults or malfunctions in bottling that allow air into the bottle. The dull, sour effects on wine of oxidation are obvious, and you should return any offending bottle to the supplier for a replacement or refund. Supermarkets in my experience are pretty good about this.

Wines that are bad because they are poorly made are a bit more complicated. You might just hate it because it's not to your taste – too sweet or too dry, too dense or too light – in which case, bad luck. But if it has classic (though now rare) faults such as mustiness, a vinegar taint (volatile acidity or acetate), cloudiness or a suspension of particles, don't drink it. Recork it and take it back to the supplier.

Glass action

There is something like a consensus in the wine world about the right kind of drinking glass. It should consist of a clear, tulip-shaped bowl on a comfortably long stem. You hold the glass by the stem so you can admire the colour of the wine and keep the bowl free of fingermarks. The bowl is big enough to hold a sensible quantity of wine at about half full. Good wine glasses have a fine bevelled surface at the rim of the bowl. Cheap glasses have a rolled rim that catches your lip and, I believe, materially diminishes the enjoyment of the wine.

Good wine glasses deserve care. Don't put them in the dishwasher. Over time, they'll craze. To maintain the crystal clarity of glasses wash them in hot soapy water, rinse clean with hot water and dry immediately with a glass cloth kept exclusively for this purpose. Sounds a bit nerdy maybe, but it can make all the difference.

What to eat with it?

When tasting a hundred or more wines one after the other and trying to make lucid notes on each of them, the mind can crave diversion. Besides describing the appearance, aroma and taste, as I'm supposed to do, I often muse on what sort of food the wine might suit.

Some of these whimsical observations make it into the finished reports for this book. Like all the rest of it, they are my own subjective opinion, but maybe they help set the wines in some sort of context.

Conventions such as white wine with fish and red with meat might be antiquated, but they can still inhibit choice. If you only like white wine must you abstain on carnivorous occasions – or go veggie? Obviously not. Much better to give detailed thought to the possibilities, and go in for plenty of experimentation.

Ripe whites from grapes such as Chardonnay can match all white meats, cured meats and barbecued meats, and most saucy meat dishes too. With bloody chunks of red meat, exotic whites from the Rhône Valley or Alsace or oaky Rioja Blanco all come immediately to mind.

As for those who prefer red wine at all times, there are few fish dishes that spurn everything red. Maybe a crab salad or a grilled Dover sole. But as soon as you add sauce, red's back on the menu. Again, the answer is to experiment.

Some foods do present particular difficulties. Nibbles such as salty peanuts or vinegary olives will clash with most table wines. So buy some proper dry sherry, chill it down and thrill to the world's best aperitif. Fino, manzanilla and amontillado sherries of real quality now feature in all the best supermarkets – some under own labels.

Eggs are supposed to be inimical to wine. Boiled, fried or poached certainly. But an omelette with a glass of wine, of any colour, is surely a match. Salads, especially those with fruit or tomatoes, get the thumbs-down, but I think it's the dressing. Forgo the vinegar, and salad opens up a vinous vista.

Cheese is a conundrum. Red wine goes with cheese, right? But soft cheeses, particularly goat's, can make red wines taste awfully tinny. You're much better off with an exotic and ripe white wine. Sweet white wines make a famously savoury match with blue cheeses. A better match, I believe, than with their conventional companions, puddings. Hard cheeses such as Cheddar may be fine with some red wines, but even better with a glass of Port.

Wine with curry? Now that incendiary dishes are entirely integrated into the national diet, I suppose this is, uh, a burning question. Big, ripe reds such as Australian Shiraz can stand up to Indian heat, and Argentine Malbec seems appropriate for chilli dishes. Chinese cuisine likes aromatic white wines such as Alsace (or New Zealand) Gewürztraminer, and salsa dishes call for zingy dry whites such as Sauvignon Blanc.

But everyone to their own taste. If there's one universal convention in food and wine matching it must surely be to suit yourself.

—A Wine Vocabulary—

A brief guide to the use of language across the wine world – on labels, in literature and among the listings in this book

---
A

AC – *See* Appellation d'Origine Contrôlée.

acidity – Natural acids in grape juice are harnessed by the winemaker to produce clean, crisp flavours. Excess acidity creates rawness or greenness; shortage is indicated by wateriness.

aftertaste – The flavour that lingers in the mouth after swallowing or spitting the wine.

Aglianico – Black grape variety of southern Italy. Vines originally planted by ancient Greek settlers from 600BC in the arid volcanic landscapes of Basilicata and Cilento produce distinctive dark and earthy reds.

Agriculture biologique – On French wine labels, an indication that the wine has been made by organic methods.

Albariño – White grape variety of Spain that makes intriguingly perfumed fresh and tangy dry wines, especially in esteemed Atlantic-facing Rias Baixas region.

alcohol – The alcohol levels in wines are expressed in terms of alcohol by volume ('abv'), that is, the percentage of the volume of the wine that is common, or ethyl, alcohol. A typical wine at 12 per cent abv is thus 12 parts alcohol and, in effect, 88 parts fruit juice. Alcohol is viewed by some health professionals as a poison, but there is actuarial evidence that total abstainers live shorter lives than moderate consumers. The UK Department of Health declares there is no safe level of alcohol consumption, and advises that drinkers should not exceed a weekly number of 'units' of alcohol. A unit is 10ml of pure alcohol, the quantity contained in about half a 175ml glass of wine with 12 per cent alcohol. From 1995, the advisory limit on weekly units was 28 for men and 21 for women. This was reduced in 2016 to 14 for men and women alike.

Alentejo – Wine region of southern Portugal (immediately north of the Algarve), with a fast-improving reputation, especially for sappy, keen reds from local grape varieties including Aragones, Castelão and Trincadeira.

Almansa – DO winemaking region of Spain inland from Alicante, making inexpensive red wines.

Alsace – France's easternmost wine-producing region lies between the Vosges Mountains and the River Rhine, with Germany beyond.

These conditions make for the production of some of the world's most delicious and fascinating white wines, always sold under the name of their constituent grapes. Pinot Blanc is the most affordable – and is well worth looking out for. The 'noble' grape varieties of the region are Gewürztraminer, Muscat, Riesling and Pinot Gris and they are always made on a single-variety basis. The richest, most exotic wines are those from individual *grand cru* vineyards, which are named on the label. Some *vendange tardive* (late harvest) wines are made, and tend to be expensive. All the wines are sold in tall, slim green bottles known as flûtes that closely resemble those of the Mosel. The names of producers as well as grape varieties are often German too, so it is widely assumed that Alsace wines are German in style, if not in nationality. But this is not the case in either particular. Alsace wines are dry and quite unique in character – and definitely French.

amarone – Style of red wine made in Valpolicella, Italy. Specially selected grapes are held back from the harvest and stored for several months to dry them out. They are then pressed and fermented into a highly concentrated speciality dry wine. Amarone means 'bitter', describing the dry style of the flavour.

amontillado – *See* sherry.

aperitif – If a wine is thus described, I believe it will give as much pleasure before a meal as with one. Crisp, low-alcohol German wines and other delicately flavoured whites (including many dry Italians) are examples.

appassimento – Italian technique of drying out new-picked grapes to concentrate the sugars. Varying proportions of appassimento fruit are added to the fermentation of speciality wines such as amarone and ripasso.

Appellation d'Origine Contrôlée – Commonly abbreviated to AC or AOC, this is the system under which top-quality wines have been defined in France since 1935. About a third of the country's vast annual output qualifies across about 500 AC (or AOP – see Appellation d'Origine Protégée) zones. The declaration of an AC on the label signifies that the wine meets standards concerning location of vineyards and wineries, grape varieties and limits on harvest per hectare, methods of cultivation and vinification, and alcohol content. Wines are inspected and tasted by state-appointed committees.

Appellation d'Origine Protégée (AOP) – Under European Union rule changes, the AOC system is gradually transforming into AOP. In effect, it means little more than the exchange of 'controlled' with 'protected' on labels. One quirk of the rules is that makers of AOP wines will be able to name the constituent grape variety or varieties on their labels, if they so wish.

Apulia – Anglicised name for Puglia, Italy.

Aragones – Synonym in Portugal, especially in the Alentejo region, for the Tempranillo grape variety of Spain.

Ardèche – Region of southern France to the west of the Rhône river, home to a good IGP zone including the Coteaux de l'Ardèche. Decent-value reds from Syrah and Cabernet Sauvignon grapes, and less interesting dry whites.

Arneis – White grape variety of Piedmont, north-west Italy. Makes dry whites with a certain almondy richness at often-inflated prices.

Assyrtiko – White grape variety of Greece now commonly named on dry white wines, sometimes of great quality, from the mainland and islands.

Asti – Town and major winemaking centre in Piedmont, Italy. The sparkling (spumante) wines made from Moscato grapes are inexpensive and sweet with a modest 5 to 7 per cent alcohol. Vivid red wine Barbera d'Asti also produced.

attack – In wine-tasting, the first impression made by the wine in the mouth.

Auslese – German wine-quality designation. *See* QmP.

B

Baga – Black grape variety indigenous to Portugal. Makes famously concentrated, juicy reds of deep colour from the grapes' particularly thick skins. Look out for this name, now quite frequently quoted as the varietal on Portuguese wine labels.

balance – A big word in the vocabulary of wine tasting. Respectable wine must get two key things right: lots of fruitiness from the sweet grape juice, and plenty of acidity so the sweetness is 'balanced' with the crispness familiar in good dry whites and the dryness that marks good reds. Some wines are noticeably 'well balanced' in that they have memorable fruitiness and the clean, satisfying 'finish' (last flavour in the mouth) that ideal acidity imparts.

Barbera – Black grape variety originally of Piedmont in Italy. Most commonly seen as Barbera d'Asti, the vigorously fruity red wine made around Asti – once better known for sweet sparkling Asti Spumante. Barbera grapes are now cultivated in South America, producing less-interesting wine than at home in Italy.

Bardolino – Once fashionable, light red wine DOC of Veneto, north-west Italy. Bardolino is made principally from Corvina Veronese grapes plus Rondinella, Molinara and Negrara. Best wines are supposed to be those labelled Bardolino Superiore, a DOCG created in 2002. This classification closely specifies the permissible grape varieties and sets the alcohol level at a minimum of 12 per cent.

Barossa Valley – Famed vineyard region north of Adelaide, Australia, produces hearty reds principally from Shiraz, Cabernet Sauvignon and Grenache grapes, plus plenty of lush white wine from Chardonnay. Also known for limey, long-lived, mineral dry whites from Riesling grapes.

barrique – Barrel in French. *En barrique* on a wine label signifies the wine has been matured in casks rather than tanks.

Beaujolais – Unique red wines from the southern reaches of Burgundy, France, are made from Gamay grapes. Beaujolais nouveau, now unfashionable, provides a friendly introduction to the bouncy, red-fruit style of the wine, but for the authentic experience, go for Beaujolais Villages, from the region's better, northern vineyards. There are ten AC zones within this northern sector making wines under their own names. Known as the *crus*, these are Brouilly, Chénas, Chiroubles, Côte de Brouilly,

Fleurie, Juliénas, Morgon, Moulin à Vent, Regnié and St Amour. Prices are higher than those for Beaujolais Villages, but not always justifiably so.

Beaumes de Venise – Village near Châteauneuf du Pape in France's Rhône valley, famous for sweet and alcoholic wine from Muscat grapes. Delicious, grapey wines. A small number of growers also make strong (sometimes rather tough) red wines under the village name.

Beaune – One of the two centres (the other is Nuits St Georges) of the Côte d'Or, the winemaking heart of Burgundy in France. Three of the region's humbler appellations take the name of the town: Côtes de Beaune, Côtes de Beaune Villages and Hautes Côtes de Beaune.

berry fruit – Some red wines deliver a burst of flavour in the mouth that corresponds to biting into a newly picked berry – strawberry, blackberry, etc. So a wine described as having berry fruit (by this writer, anyway) has freshness, liveliness and immediate appeal.

bianco – White wine, Italy.

Bical – White grape variety principally of Dão region of northern Portugal. Not usually identified on labels, because most of it goes into inexpensive sparkling wines. Can make still wines of very refreshing crispness.

biodynamics – A cultivation method taking the organic approach several steps further. Biodynamic winemakers plant and tend their vineyards according to a date and time calendar 'in harmony' with the movements of the planets. Some of France's best-known wine estates subscribe, and many more are going that way. It might all sound bonkers, but it's salutary to learn that biodynamics is based on principles first described by the eminent Austrian educationist Rudolph Steiner.

bite – In wine-tasting, the impression on the palate of a wine with plenty of acidity and, often, tannin.

blanc – White wine, France.

blanc de blancs – White wine from white grapes, France. May seem to be stating the obvious, but some white wines (e.g. champagne) are made, partially or entirely, from black grapes.

blanc de noirs – White wine from black grapes, France. Usually sparkling (especially champagne) made from black Pinot Meunier and Pinot Noir grapes, with no Chardonnay or other white varieties.

blanco – White wine, Spain and Portugal.

Blauer Zweigelt – Black grape variety of Austria, making a large proportion of the country's red wines, some of excellent quality.

Bobal – Black grape variety mostly of south-eastern Spain. Thick skin is good for colour and juice contributes acidity to blends.

bodega – In Spain, a wine producer or wine shop.

Bonarda – Black grape variety of northern Italy. Now more widely planted in Argentina, where it makes some well-regarded red wines.

botrytis – Full name, *botrytis cinerea*, is that of a beneficent fungus that can attack ripe grape bunches late in the season, shrivelling the berries to a gruesome-looking mess, which yields concentrated juice of prized sweetness. Cheerfully known as 'noble rot', this fungus is actively encouraged by winemakers in regions as diverse as Sauternes (in Bordeaux),

Monbazillac (in Bergerac), the Rhine and Mosel valleys, Hungary's Tokaji region and South Australia to make ambrosial dessert wines.

bouncy – The feel in the mouth of a red wine with young, juicy fruitiness. Good Beaujolais is bouncy, as are many north-west-Italian wines from Barbera and Dolcetto grapes.

Bourgogne Grand Ordinaire – Former AC of Burgundy, France. *See* Coteaux Bourguignons.

Bourgueil – Appellation of Loire Valley, France. Long-lived red wines from Cabernet Franc grapes.

briary – In wine tasting, associated with the flavours of fruit from prickly bushes such as blackberries.

brûlé – Pleasant burnt-toffee taste or smell, as in crème brûlée.

brut – Driest style of sparkling wine. Originally French, for very dry champagnes specially developed for the British market, but now used for sparkling wines from all round the world.

Buzet – Little-seen AC of south-west France overshadowed by Bordeaux but producing some characterful ripe reds.

C

Cabardès – AC for red and rosé wines from area north of Carcassonne, Aude, France. Principally Cabernet Sauvignon and Merlot grapes.

Cabernet Franc – Black grape variety originally of France. It makes the light-bodied and keenly edged red wines of the Loire Valley – such as Chinon and Saumur. And it is much grown in Bordeaux, especially in the appellation of St Emilion. Also now planted in Argentina, Australia and North America. Wines, especially in the Loire, are characterised by a leafy, sappy style and bold fruitiness. Most are best enjoyed young.

Cabernet Sauvignon – Black (or, rather, blue) grape variety now grown in virtually every wine-producing nation. When perfectly ripened, the grapes are smaller than many other varieties and have particularly thick skins. This means that when pressed, Cabernet grapes have a high proportion of skin to juice – and that makes for wine with lots of colour and tannin. In Bordeaux, the grape's traditional home, the grandest Cabernet-based wines have always been known as *vins de garde* (wines to keep) because they take years, even decades, to evolve as the effect of all that skin extraction preserves the fruit all the way to magnificent maturity. But in today's impatient world, these grapes are exploited in modern winemaking techniques to produce the sublime flavours of mature Cabernet without having to hang around for lengthy periods awaiting maturation. While there's nothing like a fine, ten-year-old claret (and few quite as expensive), there are many excellent Cabernets from around the world that amply illustrate this grape's characteristics. Classic smells and flavours include blackcurrants, cedar wood, chocolate, tobacco – even violets.

Cahors – An AC of the Lot Valley in south-west France once famous for 'black wine'. This was a curious concoction of straightforward wine mixed with a soupy must, made by boiling up new-pressed juice to concentrate it (through evaporation) before fermentation. The myth is still perpetuated that Cahors wine continues to be made in this way, but production on this basis actually ceased 150 years ago. Cahors today is no stronger, or blacker, than the wines of neighbouring appellations. Principal grape variety is Malbec, known locally as Cot.

Cairanne – Village of the appellation collectively known as the Côtes du Rhône in southern France. Cairanne is one of several villages entitled to put their name on the labels of wines made within their AC boundary, and the appearance of this name is quite reliably an indicator of quality.

Calatayud – DO (quality wine zone) near Zaragoza in the Aragon region of northern Spain where they're making some astonishingly good wines at bargain prices, mainly reds from Garnacha and Tempranillo grapes. These are the varieties that go into the polished and oaky wines of Rioja, but in Calatayud, the wines are dark, dense and decidedly different.

Cannonau – Black grape native to Sardinia by name, but in fact the same variety as the ubiquitous Grenache of France (and Garnacha of Spain).

cantina sociale – *See* co-op.

Carignan – Black grape variety of Mediterranean France. It is rarely identified on labels, but is a major constituent of wines from the southern Rhône and Languedoc-Roussillon regions. Known as Carignano in Italy and Cariñena in Spain.

Cariñena – A region of north-east Spain, south of Navarra, known for substantial reds, as well as the Spanish name for the Carignan grape (*qv*).

Carmenère – Black grape variety once widely grown in Bordeaux but abandoned due to cultivation problems. Lately revived in South America where it is producing fine wines, sometimes with echoes of Bordeaux.

cassis – As a tasting note, signifies a wine that has a noticeable blackcurrant-concentrate flavour or smell. Much associated with the Cabernet Sauvignon grape.

Castelao – Portuguese black grape variety. Same as Periquita.

Catarratto – White grape variety of Sicily. In skilled hands it can make anything from keen, green-fruit dry whites to lush, oaked super-ripe styles. Also used for Marsala.

cat's pee – In tasting notes, a jocular reference to the smell of a certain style of Sauvignon Blanc wine.

cava – The sparkling wine of Spain. Most originates in Catalonia, but the Denominación de Origen (DO) guarantee of authenticity is open to producers in many regions of the country. Much cava is very reasonably priced even though it is made by the same method as champagne – second fermentation in bottle, known in Spain as the *método clásico*.

CdR – Côtes du Rhône. My own shorthand.

cépage – Grape variety, French. 'Cépage Merlot' on a label simply means the wine is made largely or exclusively from Merlot grapes.

Chablis – Northernmost AC of France's Burgundy region. Its dry white wines from Chardonnay grapes are known for their fresh and steely style, but the best wines also age very gracefully into complex classics.

Chambourcin – Sounds like a cream cheese but it's a relatively modern (1963) French hybrid black grape that makes some good non-appellation lightweight-but-concentrated reds in the Loire Valley and now some heftier versions in Australia.

champagne – The sparkling wine of the strictly defined Champagne region of France, made by the equally strictly defined champagne method.

Chardonnay – Possibly the world's most popular grape variety. Said to originate from the village of Chardonnay in the Mâconnais region of southern Burgundy, the vine is now planted in every wine-producing nation. Wines are commonly characterised by generous colour and sweet-apple smell, but styles range from lean and sharp to opulently rich. Australia started the craze for oaked Chardonnay, the gold-coloured, super-ripe, buttery 'upfront' wines that are a caricature of lavish and outrageously expensive burgundies such as Meursault and Puligny-Montrachet. Rich to the point of egginess, these Aussie pretenders are now giving way to a sleeker, more minerally style with much less oak presence – if any at all. California and Chile, New Zealand and South Africa are competing hard to imitate the Burgundian style, and Australia's success in doing so.

Châteauneuf du Pape – Famed appellation centred on a picturesque village of the southern Rhône valley in France where in the 1320s French Pope Clement V had a splendid new château built for himself as a summer retreat amidst his vineyards. The red wines of the AC, which can be made from 13 different grape varieties but principally Grenache, Syrah and Mourvèdre, are regarded as the best of the southern Rhône and have become rather expensive – but they can be sensationally good. Expensive white wines are also made.

Chenin Blanc – White grape variety of the Loire Valley, France. Now also grown farther afield, especially in South Africa. Makes dry, soft white wines and also rich, sweet styles.

cherry – In wine tasting, either a pale red colour or, more commonly, a smell or flavour akin to the sun-warmed, bursting sweet ripeness of cherries. Many Italian wines, from lightweights such as Bardolino and Valpolicella to serious Chianti, have this character. 'Black cherry' as a description is often used of Merlot wines – meaning they are sweet but have a firmness of mouthfeel associated with the thicker skins of black cherries.

Cinsault – Black grape variety of southern France, where it is invariably blended with others in wines of all qualities from country reds to pricy appellations such as Châteauneuf du Pape. Also much planted in South Africa. The effect in wine is to add keen aromas (sometimes compared with turpentine) and softness to the blend. The name is often spelt Cinsaut.

Clape, La – A small *cru* (defined quality-vineyard area) within the Coteaux du Languedoc where the growers make some seriously delicious red wines, mainly from Carignan, Grenache and Syrah grapes. A name worth looking out for on labels from the region.

claret – The red wine of Bordeaux, France. Old British nickname from Latin *clarus*, meaning 'clear', recalling a time when the red wines of the region were much lighter in colour than they are now.

clarete – On Spanish labels indicates a pale-coloured red wine. Tinto signifies a deeper hue.

classed growth – English translation of French *cru classé* describes a group of 60 individual wine estates in the Médoc district of Bordeaux, which in 1855 were granted this new status on the basis that their wines were the most expensive of the day. The classification was a promotional wheeze to attract attention to the Bordeaux stand at that year's Great Exhibition in Paris. Amazingly, all of the wines concerned are still in production and most still occupy more or less their original places in the pecking order price-wise. The league was divided up into five divisions from *Premier Grand Cru Classé* (just four wines originally, with one promoted in 1971 – the only change ever made to the classification) to *Cinquième Grand Cru Classé*. Other regions of Bordeaux, notably Graves and St Emilion, have since imitated Médoc and introduced their own rankings of *cru classé* estates.

classic – An overused term in every respect – wine descriptions being no exception. In this book, the word is used to describe a very good wine of its type. So, a 'classic' Cabernet Sauvignon is one that is recognisably and admirably characteristic of that grape.

Classico – Under Italy's wine laws, this word appended to the name of a DOC or DOCG zone has an important significance. The classico wines of the region can only be made from vineyards lying in the best-rated areas, and wines thus labelled (e.g. Chianti Classico, Soave Classico, Valpolicella Classico) can be reliably counted on to be a cut above the rest.

Colombard – White grape variety of southern France. Once employed almost entirely for making the wine that is distilled for armagnac and cognac brandies, but lately restored to varietal prominence in the Côtes de Gascogne where high-tech wineries turn it into a fresh and crisp, if unchallenging, dry wine at a budget price. But beware, cheap Colombard (especially from South Africa) can still be very dull.

Conca de Barbera – Winemaking region of Catalonia, Spain.

co-op – Very many of France's good-quality, inexpensive wines are made by co-operatives. These are wine-producing centres whose members, and joint-owners, are local *vignerons* (vine growers). Each year they sell their harvests to the co-op for turning into branded wines. In Italy, co-op wines can be identified by the words *Cantina Sociale* on the label and in Germany by the term *Winzergenossenschaft*.

Corbières – A name to look out for. It's an AC of France's Midi (deep south) and produces countless robust reds and a few interesting whites, often at bargain prices.

Cortese – White grape variety of Piedmont, Italy. At its best, makes delicious, keenly brisk and fascinating wines, including those of the Gavi DOCG. Worth seeking out.

Costières de Nîmes – Until 1989, this AC of southern France was known as the Costières de Gard. It forms a buffer between the southern Rhône and Languedoc-Roussillon regions, and makes wines from broadly the same range of grape varieties. It's a name to look out for, the best red wines being notable for their concentration of colour and fruit, with the earthy-spiciness of the better Rhône wines and a likeable liquorice note. A few good white wines, too, and even a decent rosé or two.

Côte – In French, it simply means a side, or slope, of a hill. The implication in wine terms is that the grapes come from a vineyard ideally situated for maximum sunlight, good drainage and the unique soil conditions prevailing on the hill in question. It's fair enough to claim that vines grown on slopes might get more sunlight than those grown on the flat, but there is no guarantee whatsoever that any wine labelled 'Côtes du' this or that is made from grapes grown on a hillside anyway. Côtes du Rhône wines are a case in point. Many 'Côtes' wines come from entirely level vineyards and it is worth remembering that many of the vineyards of Bordeaux, producing most of the world's priciest wines, are little short of prairie-flat. The quality factor is determined much more significantly by the weather and the talents of the winemaker.

Coteaux Bourguignons – Generic AC of Burgundy, France, since 2011 for red and rosé wines from Pinot Noir and Gamay grapes, and white wines from (principally) Chardonnay and Bourgogne Aligoté grapes. The AC replaces the former appellation Bourgogne Grand Ordinaire.

Côtes de Blaye – Appellation Contrôlée zone of Bordeaux on the right bank of the River Gironde, opposite the more prestigious Médoc zone of the left bank. Best-rated vineyards qualify for the AC Premières Côtes de Blaye. A couple of centuries ago, Blaye (pronounced 'bligh') was the grander of the two, and even today makes some wines that compete well for quality, and at a fraction of the price of wines from its more fashionable rival across the water.

Côtes de Bourg – AC neighbouring Côtes de Blaye, making red wines of decent quality and value.

Côtes du Luberon – Appellation Contrôlée zone of Provence in south-east France. Wines, mostly red, are similar in style to Côtes du Rhône.

Côtes du Rhône – One of the biggest and best-known appellations of south-east France, covering an area roughly defined by the southern reaches of the valley of the River Rhône. The Côtes du Rhône AC achieves notably consistent quality at all points along the price scale. Lots of brilliant-value warm and spicy reds, principally from Grenache and Syrah grapes. There are also some white and rosé wines.

Côtes du Rhône Villages – Appellation within the larger Côtes du Rhône AC for wine of supposed superiority made in a number of zones associated with a long list of nominated individual villages.

Côtes du Roussillon – Huge appellation of south-west France known for strong, dark, peppery reds often offering very decent value.

Côtes du Roussillon Villages – Appellation for superior wines from a number of nominated locations within the larger Roussillon AC. Some of these village wines can be of exceptional quality and value.

crianza – Means 'nursery' in Spanish. On Rioja and Navarra wines, the designation signifies a wine that has been nursed through a maturing period of at least a year in oak casks and a further six months in bottle before being released for sale.

cru – A word that crops up with confusing regularity on French wine labels. It means 'the growing' or 'the making' of a wine and asserts that the wine concerned is from a specific vineyard. Under the Appellation Contrôlée rules, countless *crus* are classified in various hierarchical ranks. Hundreds of individual vineyards are described as *premier cru* or *grand cru* in the classic wine regions of Alsace, Bordeaux, Burgundy and Champagne. The common denominator is that the wine can be counted on to be expensive. On humbler wines, the use of the word *cru* tends to be mere decoration.

cru classé – *See* classed growth.

cuve – A vat for wine. French.

cuvée – French for the wine in a *cuve*, or vat. The word is much used on labels to imply that the wine is from just one vat, and thus of unique, unblended character. *Première cuvée* is supposedly the best wine from a given pressing because it comes from the free-run juice of grapes crushed by their own weight before pressing begins. Subsequent *cuvées* will have been from harsher pressings, grinding the grape pulp to extract the last drops of juice.

D

Dão – Major wine-producing region of northern Portugal now turning out much more interesting reds than it used to – worth looking out for anything made by mega-producer Sogrape.

demi sec – 'Half-dry' style of French (and some other) wines. Beware. It can mean anything from off-dry to cloyingly sweet.

DO – Denominación de Origen, Spain's wine-regulating scheme, similar to France's AC, but older – the first DO region was Rioja, from 1926. DO wines are Spain's best, accounting for a third of the nation's annual production.

DOC – Stands for Denominazione di Origine Controllata, Italy's equivalent of France's AC. The wines are made according to the stipulations of each of the system's 300-plus denominated zones of origin, along with a further 74 zones, which enjoy the superior classification of DOCG (DOC with *e Garantita* – guaranteed – appended).

DOCa – *Denominación de Origen Calificada* is Spain's highest regional wine classification; currently only Priorat and Rioja qualify.

DOP – Denominazione di Origine Protetta is an alternative classification to DOC (*qv*) under EU directive in Italy, comparable to AOP (*qv*) in France, but not yet widely adopted.

Durif – Rare black grape variety mostly of California, where it is also known as Petite Sirah, with some plantings in Australia.

E

earthy – A tricky word in the wine vocabulary. In this book, its use is meant to be complimentary. It indicates that the wine somehow suggests the soil the grapes were grown in, even (perhaps a shade too poetically) the landscape in which the vineyards lie. The amazing-value red wines of the torrid, volcanic southernmost regions of Italy are often described as earthy. This is an association with the pleasantly 'scorched' back-flavour in wines made from the ultra-ripe harvests of this near-sub-tropical part of the world.

edge – A wine with edge is one with evident (although not excessive) acidity.

élevé – 'Brought up' in French. Much used on wine labels where the wine has been matured (brought up) in oak barrels, *élevé en fûts de chêne*, to give it extra dimensions.

Entre Deux Mers – Meaning 'between two seas', it's a region lying between the Dordogne and Garonne rivers of Bordeaux, now mainly known for dry white wines from Sauvignon Blanc and Semillon grapes.

Estremadura – Wine-producing region occupying Portugal's coastal area north of Lisbon. Lots of interesting wines from indigenous grape varieties, often at bargain prices. If a label mentions Estremadura, it is a safe rule that there might be something good within.

Extremadura – Minor wine-producing region of western Spain abutting the frontier with Portugal's Alentejo region. Not to be confused with Estremadura of Portugal (above).

F

Falanghina – Revived ancient grape variety of southern Italy now making some superbly fresh and tangy white wines.

Faugères – AC of the Languedoc in south-west France. Source of many hearty, economic reds.

Feteasca – White grape variety widely grown in Romania. Name means 'maiden's grape' and the wine tends to be soft and slightly sweet.

Fiano – White grape variety of the Campania of southern Italy and Sicily, lately revived. It is said to have been cultivated by the ancient Romans for a wine called Apianum.

finish – The last flavour lingering in the mouth after wine has been swallowed.

fino – Pale and very dry style of sherry. You drink it thoroughly chilled – and you don't keep it any longer after opening than other dry white wines. Needs to be fresh to be at its best.

Fitou – AC of Languedoc, France. Red wines principally from Carignan, Grenache, Mourvèdre and Syrah grapes.

flabby – Fun word describing a wine that tastes dilute or watery, with insufficient acidity.

Frappato – Black grape variety of Sicily. Light red wines.

fruit – In tasting terms, the fruit is the greater part of the overall flavour of a wine. The wine is, after all, composed entirely of fruit

G

Gamay – The black grape that makes all red Beaujolais and some ordinary burgundy. It is a pretty safe rule to avoid Gamay wines from other regions.

Garganega – White grape variety of the Veneto region of north-east Italy. Best known as the principal ingredient of Soave, but occasionally included in varietal blends and mentioned as such on labels. Correctly pronounced 'gar-GAN-iga'.

Garnacha – Spanish black grape variety synonymous with Grenache of France. It is blended with Tempranillo to make the red wines of Rioja and Navarra, and is now quite widely cultivated elsewhere in Spain to make grippingly fruity varietals.

garrigue – Arid land of France's deep south giving its name to a style of red wine that notionally evokes the herby, heated, peppery flavours associated with such a landscape and its flora. A tricky metaphor.

Gavi – DOCG for dry aromatic white wine from Cortese grapes in Piedmont, north-west Italy. Trendy Gavi di Gavi wines tend to be enjoyably lush, but are rather expensive.

Gewürztraminer – One of the great grape varieties of Alsace, France. At their best, the wines are perfumed with lychees and are richly, spicily fruity, yet quite dry. Gewürztraminer from Alsace can be expensive, but the grape is also grown with some success in Germany, Italy, New Zealand and South America, at more approachable prices. Pronounced 'ge-VOORTS-traminner'.

Givry – AC for red and white wines in the Côte Chalonnaise sub-region of Burgundy. Source of some wonderfully natural-tasting reds that might be lighter than those of the more prestigious Côte d'Or to the north, but have great merits of their own. Relatively, the wines are often underpriced.

Glera – New official name for the Prosecco grape of northern Italy.

Godello – White grape variety of Galicia, Spain.

Graciano – Black grape variety of Spain that is one of the minor constituents of Rioja. Better known in its own right in Australia where it can make dense, spicy, long-lived red wines.

green – I don't often use this in the pejorative. Green, to me, is a likeable degree of freshness, especially in Sauvignon Blanc wines.

Grecanico – White grape variety of southern Italy, especially Sicily. Aromatic, grassy dry white wines.

Greco – White grape variety of southern Italy believed to be of ancient Greek origin. Big-flavoured dry white wines.

Grenache – The mainstay of the wines of the southern Rhône Valley in France. Grenache is usually the greater part of the mix in Côtes du Rhône reds and is widely planted right across the neighbouring Languedoc-Roussillon region. It's a big-cropping variety that thrives even in the hottest climates and is really a blending grape – most commonly with Syrah, the noble variety of the northern Rhône. Few French wines are labelled with its name, but the grape has caught on in Australia in a big way and it is now becoming a familiar varietal, known for strong, dark liquorous reds. Grenache is the French name for what is originally a Spanish variety, Garnacha.

Grillo – White grape of Sicily said to be among the island's oldest indigenous varieties, pre-dating the arrival of the Greeks in 600 BC. Much used for fortified Marsala, it has lately been revived for interesting, aromatic dry table wines.

grip – In wine-tasting terminology, the sensation in the mouth produced by a wine that has a healthy quantity of tannin in it. A wine with grip is a good wine. A wine with too much tannin, or which is still too young (the tannin hasn't 'softened' with age) is not described as having grip, but as mouth-puckering – or simply undrinkable.

Grolleau – Black grape variety of the Loire Valley principally cultivated for Rosé d'Anjou.

Gros Plant – White grape variety of the Pays Nantais in France's Loire estuary; synonymous with the Folle Blanche grape of south-west France.

Grüner Veltliner – The 'national' white-wine grape of Austria. In the past it made mostly soft, German-style everyday wines, but now is behind some excellent dry styles, too.

H

halbtrocken – 'Half-dry' in Germany's wine vocabulary. A reassurance that the wine is not a sugared Liebfraumilch-style confection.

hard – In red wine, a flavour denoting excess tannin, probably due to immaturity.

Haut-Médoc – Extensive AC of Bordeaux accounting for the greater part of the vineyard area to the north of the city of Bordeaux west of the Gironde river. The Haut-Médoc incorporates the prestigious commune-ACs of Listrac, Margaux, Moulis, Pauillac, St Estèphe and St Julien.

Hermitage – AC of northern Rhône Valley, France for red wines from Syrah grapes and some whites. Hermitage is also the regional name in South Africa for the Cinsaut grape.

hock – The wine of Germany's Rhine river valleys. Traditionally, but no longer consistently, it comes in brown bottles, as distinct from the wine of the Mosel river valleys – which comes in green ones.

Hunter Valley – Long-established (1820s) wine-producing region of New South Wales, Australia.

I

Indicación Geográfica Protegida (IGP) – Spain's country-wine quality designation covers 46 zones across the country. Wines made under the IGP can be labelled Vino de la Tierra.

Indication Géographique Protégée (IGP) – Introduced to France in 2010 under EU-wide wine-designation rules, IGP covers the wines previously known as vins de pays. Some wines are currently labelled IGP, but established vins de pays producers are redesignating slowly, if at all, and are not obliged to do so. Some will abbreviate, so, for example, Vin de Pays d'Oc shortens to Pays d'Oc.

Indicazione Geografica Tipica (IGT) – Italian wine-quality designation, broadly equivalent to France's IGP. The label has to state the geographical location of the vineyard and will often (but not always) state the principal grape varieties from which the wine is made.

isinglass – A gelatinous material used in fining (clarifying) wine. It is derived from fish bladders and consequently is eschewed by makers of 'vegetarian' or 'vegan' wines.

J

jammy – The 'sweetness' in dry red wines is supposed to evoke ripeness rather than sugariness. Sometimes, flavours include a sweetness reminiscent of jam. Usually a fault in the winemaking technique.

Jerez – Wine town of Andalucia, Spain, and home to sherry. The English word 'sherry' is a simple mispronunciation of Jerez.

joven – Young wine, Spanish. In regions such as Rioja, *vino joven* is a synonym for *sin crianza*, which means 'without ageing' in cask or bottle.

Jura – Wine region of eastern France incorporating four AOCs, Arbois, Château-Chalon, Côtes du Jura and L'Etoile. Known for still red, white and rosé wines and sparkling wines as well as exotic *vin de paille* and *vin jaune*.

Jurançon – Appellation for white wines from Courbu and Manseng grapes at Pau, south-west France.

K

Kabinett – Under Germany's bewildering wine-quality rules, this is a classification of a top-quality (QmP) wine. Expect a keen, dry, racy style. The name comes from the cabinet or cupboard in which winemakers traditionally kept their most treasured bottles.

Kekfrankos – Black grape variety of Hungary, particularly the Sopron region, which makes some of the country's more interesting red wines, characterised by colour and spiciness. Same variety as Austria's Blaufrankisch.

L

Ladoix – Unfashionable AC at northern edge of Côtes de Beaune makes some of Burgundy's true bargain reds. A name to look out for.

Lambrusco – The name is that of a black grape variety widely grown across northern Italy. True Lambrusco wine is red, dry and very slightly sparkling, and enjoying a current vogue in Britain.

Languedoc-Roussillon – Extensive wine region of southern France incorporating numerous ACs and IGP zones, notably the Pays d'Oc and Côtes de Roussillon.

lees – The detritus of the winemaking process that collects in the bottom of the vat or cask. Wines left for extended periods on the lees can acquire extra dimensions of flavour, in particular a 'leesy' creaminess.

legs – The liquid residue left clinging to the sides of the glass after wine has been swirled. The persistence of the legs is an indicator of the weight of alcohol. Also known as 'tears'.

lieu dit – This is starting to appear on French wine labels. It translates as an 'agreed place' and is an area of vineyard defined as of particular character or merit, but not classified under wine law. Usually, the *lieu dit*'s name is stated, with the implication that the wine in question has special merit.

liquorice – The pungent, slightly burnt flavours of this confection are detectable in some wines made from very ripe grapes, for example, the Malbec harvested in Argentina and several varieties grown in the very hot vineyards of southernmost Italy. A close synonym is 'tarry'. This characteristic is by no means a fault in red wine, unless very dominant, but it can make for a challenging flavour that might not appeal to all tastes.

liquorous – Wines of great weight and glyceriney texture (evidenced by the 'legs', or 'tears', which cling to the glass after the wine has been swirled) are always noteworthy. The connection with liquor is drawn in respect of the feel of the wine in the mouth, rather than with the higher alcoholic strength of spirits.

Lirac – Village and AC of southern Rhône Valley, France. A near-neighbour of the esteemed appellation of Châteauneuf du Pape, Lirac makes red wine of comparable depth and complexity, at competitive prices.

Lugana – DOC of Lombardy, Italy, known for a dry white wine that is often of real distinction – rich, almondy stuff from the ubiquitous Trebbiano grape.

M

Macabeo – One of the main grapes used for cava, the sparkling wine of Spain. It is the same grape as Viura.

Mâcon – Town and collective appellation of southern Burgundy, France. Minerally white wines from Chardonnay grapes and light reds from Pinot Noir and some Gamay. The better ones, and the ones exported, have the AC Mâcon-Villages and there are individual village wines with their own ACs including Mâcon-Clessé, Mâcon-Viré and Mâcon-Lugny.

Malbec – Black grape variety grown on a small scale in Bordeaux, and the mainstay of the wines of Cahors in France's Dordogne region under the name Cot. Now much better known for producing big butch reds in Argentina.

malolactic fermentation – In winemaking, a common natural bacterial action following alcoholic fermentation, converting malic (apple) acid into lactic (milk) acid. The effect is to reduce tartness and to boost creaminess in the wine. Adding lactic bacteria to wine to promote the process is widely practised.

manzanilla – Pale, very dry sherry of Sanlucar de Barrameda, a resort town on the Bay of Cadiz in Spain. Manzanilla is proud to be distinct from the pale, very dry fino sherry of the main producing town of Jerez de la Frontera an hour's drive inland. Drink it chilled and fresh – it goes downhill in an opened bottle after just a few days, even if kept (as it should be) in the fridge.

Margaret River – Vineyard region of Western Australia regarded as ideal for grape varieties including Cabernet Sauvignon. It has a relatively cool climate and a reputation for making sophisticated wines, both red and white.

Marlborough – Best-known vineyard region of New Zealand's South Island has a cool climate and a name for brisk but cerebral Sauvignon Blanc and Chardonnay wines.

Marsanne – White grape variety of the northern Rhône Valley and, increasingly, of the wider south of France. It's known for making well-coloured wines with heady aroma and nuanced fruit.

Mataro – Black grape variety of Australia. It's the same as the Mourvèdre of France and Monastrell of Spain.

Mazuelo – Spanish name for France's black grape variety Carignan.

McLaren Vale – Vineyard region south of Adelaide in south-east Australia. Known for blockbuster Shiraz (and Chardonnay) that can be of great balance and quality from winemakers who manage to keep the ripeness under control.

meaty – In wine-tasting, a weighty, rich red wine style.

Mencia – Black grape variety of Galicia and north-west Spain. Light red wines.

Mendoza – Wine region of Argentina. Lying to the east of the Andes mountains, just about opposite the best vineyards of Chile on the other side, Mendoza accounts for the bulk of Argentine wine production.

Merlot – One of the great black wine grapes of Bordeaux, and now grown all over the world. The name is said to derive from the French *merle*, a blackbird. Characteristics of Merlot-based wines attract descriptions such as 'plummy' and 'plump' with black-cherry aromas. The grapes are larger than most, and thus have less skin in proportion to their flesh. This means the resulting wines have less tannin than wines from smaller-berry varieties such as Cabernet Sauvignon, and are therefore, in the Bordeaux context at least, more suitable for drinking while still relatively young.

middle palate – In wine-tasting, the impression given by the wine after the first impact on 'entry' and before the 'finish' when the wine is swallowed.

Midi – Catch-all term for the deep south of France west of the Rhône Valley.

mineral – Irresistible term in wine-tasting. To me it evokes flavours such as the stone-pure freshness of some Loire dry whites, or the flinty quality of the more austere style of the Chardonnay grape, especially in Chablis. Mineral really just means something mined, as in dug out of the ground, like iron ore (as in 'steely' whites) or rock, as in, er, stone. Maybe there's something in it, but I am not entirely confident.

Minervois – AC for (mostly) red wines from vineyards around the Roman-founded town of Minerve in the Languedoc-Roussillon region of France. Often good value. The recently elevated Minervois La Livinière AC is a sort of Minervois *grand cru*.

Monastrell – Black grape variety of Spain, widely planted in Mediterranean regions for inexpensive wines notable for their high alcohol and toughness – though they can mature into excellent, soft reds. The variety is known in France as Mourvèdre and in Australia as Mataro.

Monbazillac – AC for sweet, dessert wines within the wider appellation of Bergerac in south-west France. Made from the same grape varieties (principally Sauvignon and Semillon) that go into the much costlier counterpart wines of Barsac and Sauternes near Bordeaux, these stickies from botrytis-affected, late-harvested grapes can be delicious and good value for money.

Montalcino – Hill town of Tuscany, Italy, and a DOCG for strong and very long-lived red wines from Brunello grapes. The wines are mostly very expensive. Rosso di Montalcino, a DOC for the humbler wines of the zone, is often a good buy.

Montepulciano – Black grape variety of Italy. Best known in Montepulciano d'Abruzzo, the juicy, purply-black and bramble-fruited red of the Abruzzi region midway down Italy's Adriatic side. Also the grape in the rightly popular hearty reds of Rosso Conero from around Ancona in the Marches. Not to be confused with the hill town of Montepulciano in Tuscany, famous for expensive Vino Nobile di Montepulciano wine, made from Sangiovese grapes.

morello – Lots of red wines have smells and flavours redolent of cherries. Morello cherries, among the darkest coloured and sweetest of all varieties and the preferred choice of cherry-brandy producers, have a distinct sweetness resembled by some wines made from Merlot grapes. A morello whiff or taste is generally very welcome.

Moscatel – Spanish Muscat.

Moscato – *See* Muscat.

moselle – The wine of Germany's Mosel river valleys, collectively known for winemaking purposes as the Mosel-Saar-Ruwer. The wine always comes in slim, green bottles, as distinct from the brown bottles traditionally, but no longer exclusively, employed for Rhine wines.

Mourvèdre – Widely planted black grape variety of southern France. It's an ingredient in many of the wines of Provence, the Rhône and Languedoc, including the ubiquitous Pays d'Oc. It's a hot-climate vine and the wine is usually blended with other varieties to give sweet aromas and 'backbone' to the mix. Known as Mataro in Australia and Monastrell in Spain.

Muscadet – One of France's most familiar everyday whites, made from a grape called the Melon or Melon de Bourgogne. It comes from vineyards at the estuarial end of the River Loire, and has a sea-breezy freshness about it. The better wines are reckoned to be those from the vineyards in the Sèvre et Maine region, and many are made *sur lie* – 'on the lees' – meaning that the wine is left in contact with the yeasty deposit of its fermentation until just before bottling, in an endeavour to add interest to what can sometimes be an acidic and fruitless style.

Muscat – Grape variety with origins in ancient Greece, and still grown widely among the Aegean islands for the production of sweet white wines. Muscats are the wines that taste more like grape juice than any other – but the high sugar levels ensure they are also among the most alcoholic of wines, too. Known as Moscato in Italy, the grape is much used for making sweet sparkling wines, as in Asti Spumante or Moscato d'Asti. There are several appellations in south-west France for inexpensive Muscats made rather like port, part-fermented before the addition of grape alcohol to halt the conversion of sugar into alcohol, creating a sweet and heady *vin doux naturel*. Dry Muscat wines, when well made, have a delicious sweet aroma but a refreshing, light touch with flavours reminiscent variously of orange blossom, wood smoke and grapefruit.

must – New-pressed grape juice prior to fermentation.

N

Navarra – DO wine-producing region of northern Spain adjacent to, and overshadowed by, Rioja. Navarra's wines can be startlingly akin to their neighbouring rivals, and sometimes rather better value for money.

négociant – In France, a dealer-producer who buys wines from growers and matures and/or blends them for bottling and sale under his or her own label. Purists can be a bit sniffy about these entrepreneurs, claiming that only the vine-grower with his or her own winemaking set-up can make truly authentic stuff, but the truth is that many of the best wines of France are *négociant*-produced – especially at the humbler end of the price scale. *Négociants* are often identified on wine labels as *négociant-éleveur* (literally 'dealer-bringer-up'), meaning that the wine has been matured, blended and bottled by the party in question.

Negroamaro – Black grape variety mainly of Puglia, the much-lauded wine region of south-east Italy. Dense, earthy red wines with ageing potential and plenty of alcohol. The name is probably (if not obviously) derived from Italian *negro* (black) and *amaro* (bitter). The grape behind Copertino, Salice Salentino and Squinzano.

Nerello Mascalese – Black grape of Sicily, most prolific in vineyards surrounding Mount Etna, making distinctive, flavoursome reds.

Nero d'Avola – Black grape variety of Sicily (Avola is a town in the province of Syracuse) and southern Italy. It makes deep-coloured wines that, given half a chance, can develop intensity and richness with age.

non-vintage – A wine is described as such when it has been blended from the harvests of more than one year. A non-vintage wine is not necessarily an inferior one, but under quality-control regulations around the world, still table wines most usually derive solely from one year's grape crop to qualify for appellation status. Champagnes and sparkling wines are mostly blended from several vintages, as are fortified wines such as port and sherry.

nose – In the vocabulary of the wine-taster, the nose is the scent of a wine. Sounds a bit dotty, but it makes a sensible enough alternative to the rather bald 'smell'. The use of the word 'perfume' implies that the wine smells particularly good. 'Aroma' is used specifically to describe a wine that smells as it should, as in 'this burgundy has the authentic strawberry-raspberry aroma of Pinot Noir'.

O

oak – Most of the world's costliest wines are matured in new or nearly new oak barrels, giving additional opulence of flavour. Of late, many cheaper wines have been getting the oak treatment, too, in older, cheaper casks, or simply by having sacks of oak chippings poured into their steel or fibreglass holding tanks. 'Oak aged' on a label is likely to indicate the latter treatments. But the overtly oaked wines of Australia have in some cases been so overdone that there is now a reactive trend whereby some producers proclaim their wines – particularly Chardonnays – as 'unoaked' on the label, thereby asserting that the flavours are more naturally achieved.

Oltrepo Pavese – Wine-producing zone of Piedmont, north-west Italy. The name means 'south of Pavia across the [river] Po' and the wines, both white and red, can be excellent quality and value for money.

organic wine – As in other sectors of the food industry, demand for organically made wine is – or appears to be – growing. As a rule, a wine qualifies as organic if it comes entirely from grapes grown in vineyards cultivated without the use of synthetic materials, and made in a winery where chemical treatments or additives are shunned with similar vigour. In fact, there are plenty of winemakers in the world using organic methods, but who disdain to label their bottles as such. Wines proclaiming their organic status used to carry the same sort of premium as their counterparts round the corner in the fruit, vegetable and meat aisles. But organic viticulture is now commonplace and there seems little price impact. There is no single worldwide (or even Europe-wide) standard for organic food or wine, so you pretty much have to take the producer's word for it.

P

Pasqua – One of the biggest and, it should be said, best wine producers of the Veneto region of north-west Italy.

Passerina – White grape variety of Marche, Italy. Used in blending but there is also a regional Passerina DOC.

Passetoutgrains – Designation for wine made from more than one grape variety grown in the same vineyard. French. Mostly red burgundy from Gamay and Pinot Noir.

Pays d'Oc – Shortened form under recent rule changes of French wine designation Vin de Pays d'Oc. All other similar regional designations can be similarly abbreviated.

Pecorino – White grape variety of mid-eastern Italy currently in vogue for well-coloured dry white varietal wines.

Periquita – Black grape variety of southern Portugal. Makes rather exotic spicy reds. Name means 'parrot'.

Perricone – Black grape variety of Sicily. Low-acid red wines.

PET – It's what they call plastic wine bottles – lighter to transport and allegedly as ecological as glass. Polyethylene terephthalate.

Petit Verdot – Black grape variety of Bordeaux contributing additional colour, density and spiciness to Cabernet Sauvignon-dominated blends. Mostly a minority player at home, but in Australia and California it is grown as the principal variety for some big hearty reds of real character.

petrol – When white wines from certain grapes, especially Riesling, are allowed to age in the bottle for longer than a year or two, they can take on a spirity aroma reminiscent of petrol or diesel. In grand mature German wines, this is considered a good thing.

Picpoul – Grape variety of southern France. Best known in Picpoul de Pinet, a dry white from near Sète on the Golfe de Lyon, lately elevated to AOP status. The name Picpoul (also Piquepoul) means 'stings the lips' – referring to the natural high acidity of the juice.

Piemonte – North-western province of Italy, which we call Piedmont, known for the spumante wines of the town of Asti, plus expensive Barbaresco and Barolo and better-value varietal red wines from Nebbiolo, Barbera and Dolcetto grapes.

Pinotage – South Africa's own black grape variety. Makes red wines ranging from light and juicy to dark, strong and long-lived. It's a cross between Pinot Noir and a grape the South Africans used to call Hermitage (thus the portmanteau name) but turns out to have been Cinsault.

Pinot Blanc – White grape variety principally of Alsace, France. Florally perfumed, exotically fruity dry white wines.

Pinot Grigio – White grape variety of northern Italy. Wines bearing its name are perplexingly fashionable. Good examples have an interesting smoky-pungent aroma and keen, slaking fruit. But most are dull. Originally French, it is at its best in the lushly exotic Pinot Gris wines of Alsace and is also successfully cultivated in Germany and New Zealand.

Pinot Noir – The great black grape of Burgundy, France. It makes all the region's fabulously expensive red wines. Notoriously difficult to grow in warmer climates, it is nevertheless cultivated by countless intrepid winemakers in the New World intent on reproducing the magic appeal of red burgundy. California and New Zealand have come closest. Some Chilean Pinot Noirs are inexpensive and worth trying.

Pouilly Fuissé – Village and AC of the Mâconnais region of southern Burgundy in France. Dry white wines from Chardonnay grapes. Wines are among the highest rated of the Mâconnais.

Pouilly Fumé – Village and AC of the Loire Valley in France. Dry white wines from Sauvignon Blanc grapes. Similar 'pebbly', 'grassy' or 'gooseberry' style to neighbouring AC Sancerre. The notion put about by some enthusiasts that Pouilly Fumé is 'smoky' is surely nothing more than word association with the name.

Primitivo – Black grape variety of southern Italy, especially the region of Puglia. Named from Latin *primus* for first, the grape is among the earliest-ripening of all varieties. The wines are typically dense and dark in colour with plenty of alcohol, and have an earthy, spicy style.

Priorat – Emerging wine region of Catalonia, Spain. Highly valued red wines from Garnacha and other varieties. Generic brands available in supermarkets are well worth trying out.

Prosecco – Softly sparkling wine of Italy's Veneto region. The best come from the DOCG Conegliano-Valdobbiadene, made as spumante ('foaming') wines in pressurised tanks, typically to 11 per cent alcohol and ranging from softly sweet to crisply dry. The constituent grape, previously also known as Prosecco, has been officially assigned the name Glera.

Puglia – The region occupying the 'heel' of southern Italy, making many good, inexpensive wines from indigenous grape varieties.

Q

QbA – German, standing for Qualitätswein bestimmter Anbaugebiete. It means 'quality wine from designated areas' and implies that the wine is made from grapes with a minimum level of ripeness, but it's by no means a guarantee of exciting quality. Only wines labelled QmP (see next entry) can be depended upon to be special.

QmP – Stands for Qualitätswein mit Prädikat. These are the serious wines of Germany, made without the addition of sugar to 'improve' them. To qualify for QmP status, the grapes must reach a level of ripeness as measured on a sweetness scale – all according to Germany's fiendishly complicated wine-quality regulations. Wines from grapes that reach the stated minimum level of sweetness qualify for the description of Kabinett. The next level up earns the rank of Spätlese, meaning 'late-picked'. Kabinett wines can be expected to be dry and brisk in style, and Spätlese wines a little bit riper and fuller. The next grade up, Auslese, meaning 'selected harvest', indicates a wine made from super-ripe grapes; it will be golden in colour and honeyed in flavour. A generation ago, these wines were as valued, and as expensive, as any of the world's grandest appellations. Beerenauslese and Trockenbeerenauslese are speciality wines made from individually picked late-harvest grapes.

Quincy – AC of Loire Valley, France, known for pebbly-dry white wines from Sauvignon grapes. The wines are forever compared to those of nearby and much better-known Sancerre – and Quincy often represents better value for money. Pronounced 'KAN-see'.

Quinta – Portuguese for farm or estate. It precedes the names of many of Portugal's best-known wines. It is pronounced 'KEEN-ta'.

R

racy – Evocative wine-tasting description for wine that thrills the tastebuds with a rush of exciting sensations. Good Rieslings often qualify.

raisiny – Wines from grapes that have been very ripe or overripe at harvest can take on a smell and flavour akin to the concentrated, heat-dried sweetness of raisins. As a minor element in the character of a wine, this can add to the appeal but as a dominant characteristic it is a fault.

rancio – Spanish term harking back to Roman times when wines were commonly stored in jars outside, exposed to the sun, so they oxidised and took on a burnt sort of flavour. Today, *rancio* describes a baked – and by no means unpleasant – flavour in fortified wines, particularly sherry and Madeira.

Reserva – In Portugal and Spain, this has genuine significance. The Portuguese use it for special wines with a higher alcohol level and longer ageing, although the precise periods vary between regions. In Spain, especially in the Navarra and Rioja regions, it means the wine must have had at least a year in oak and two in bottle before release.

reserve – On French (as *réserve*) or other wines, this implies special-quality, longer-aged wines, but has no official significance.

residual sugar – There is sugar in all wine, left over from the fermentation process. Some producers now mention the quantity of residual sugar on back labels in grams per litre of wine, even though so far there is no legal obligation to do so. Dry wines, red or white, typically have 3 g/l or fewer. Above that, you might well be able to taste the sweetness. In southern hemisphere wines, made from grapes that have ripened under more-intense sunlight than their European counterparts, sugar levels can be correspondingly higher. Sweet wines such as Sauternes contain up to 150 g/l. Dry ('brut') sparkling wines made by the 'champagne' method typically have 10 g/l and tank-method fizzes such as prosecco up to 15 g/l.

Retsina – The universal white wine of Greece. It has been traditionally made in Attica, the region of Athens, for a very long time, and is said to owe its origins and name to the ancient custom of sealing amphorae (terracotta jars) of the wine with a gum made from pine resin. Some of the flavour of the resin inevitably transmitted itself into the wine, and ancient Greeks acquired a lasting taste for it.

Reuilly – AC of Loire Valley, France, for crisp dry whites from Sauvignon grapes. Pronounced 'RER-yee'.

Ribatejo – Emerging wine region of Portugal. Worth seeking out on labels of red wines in particular, because new winemakers are producing lively stuff from distinctive indigenous grapes such as Castelao and Trincadeira.

Ribera del Duero – Classic wine region of north-west Spain lying along the River Duero (which crosses the border to become Portugal's Douro, forming the valley where port comes from). It is home to an estate oddly named Vega Sicilia, where red wines of epic quality are made and sold at equally epic prices. Further down the scale, some very good reds are made, too.

Riesling – The noble grape variety of Germany. It is correctly pronounced 'REEZ-ling', not 'RICE-ling'. Once notorious as the grape behind all those boring 'medium' Liebfraumilches and Niersteiners, this grape has had a bad press. In fact, there has never been much, if any, Riesling in German plonk. But the country's best wines, the so-called Qualitätswein mit Prädikat grades, are made almost exclusively with Riesling. These wines range from crisply fresh and appley styles to extravagantly fruity, honeyed wines from late-harvested grapes. Excellent Riesling wines are also made in Alsace and now in Australasia.

Rioja – The principal fine-wine region of Spain, in the country's north east. The pricier wines are noted for their vanilla-pod richness from long ageing in oak casks. Tempranillo and Garnacha grapes make the reds, Viura the whites.

Ripasso – A particular style of Valpolicella wine. New wine is partially refermented in vats that have been used to make Recioto reds (wines made from semi-dried grapes), thus creating a bigger, smoother version of usually light and pale Valpolicella.

Riserva – In Italy, a wine made only in the best vintages, and allowed longer ageing in cask and bottle.

Rivaner – Alternative name for Germany's Müller-Thurgau grape.

Riverland – Vineyard region to the immediate north of the Barossa Valley of South Australia, extending east into New South Wales.

Roditis – White grape variety of Greece, known for fresh dry whites with decent acidity, often included in retsina.

rosso – Red wine, Italy.

Rosso Conero – DOC red wine made in the environs of Ancona in the Marches, Italy. Made from the Montepulciano grape, the wine can provide excellent value for money.

Ruby Cabernet – Black grape variety of California, created by crossing Cabernet Sauvignon and Carignan. Makes soft and squelchy red wine at home and in South Africa.

Rueda – DO of north-west Spain making first-class refreshing dry whites from the indigenous Verdejo grape, imported Sauvignon, and others. Exciting quality, and prices are keen.

Rully – AC of Chalonnais region of southern Burgundy, France. White wines from Chardonnay and red wines from Pinot Noir grapes. Both can be very good and substantially cheaper than their more northerly Burgundian neighbours. Pronounced 'ROO-yee'.

S

Sagrantino – Black grape variety native to Perugia, Italy. Dark, tannic wines best known in DOCG Sagrantino de Montefalco. Now also cultivated in Australia.

Saint Emilion – AC of Bordeaux, France. Centred on the romantic hill town of St Emilion, this famous sub-region makes some of the grandest red wines of France, but also some of the best-value ones. Less fashionable than the Médoc region on the opposite (west) bank of the River Gironde that bisects Bordeaux, St Emilion wines are made largely with the Merlot grape, and are relatively quick to mature. The top wines are classified *1er grand cru classé* and are madly expensive, but many more are classified respectively *grand cru classé* and *grand cru*, and these designations can be seen as a fairly trustworthy indicator of quality. There are several 'satellite' St Emilion ACs named after the villages at their centres, notably Lussac St Emilion, Montagne St Emilion and Puisseguin St Emilion. Some excellent wines are made by estates within these ACs, and at relatively affordable prices thanks to the comparatively humble status of their satellite designations.

Salento – Up-and-coming wine region of southern Italy. Many good bargain reds from local grapes including Nero d'Avola and Primitivo.

Sancerre – AC of the Loire Valley, France, renowned for flinty-fresh Sauvignon Blanc whites and rarer Pinot Noir reds and rosés.

Sangiovese – The local black grape of Tuscany, Italy, is the principal variety used for Chianti. Also planted further south in Italy and in the New World. Generic Sangiovese di Toscana can make a consoling substitute for costly Chianti.

Saumur – Town and appellation of Loire Valley, France. Characterful minerally red wines from Cabernet Franc grapes, and some whites. Sparkling wines from Chenin Blanc grapes can be good value.

Saumur-Champigny – Separate appellation for red wines from Cabernet Franc grapes of Saumur in the Loire, sometimes very good and lively.

Sauvignon Blanc – French white grape variety now grown worldwide. New Zealand has raised worldwide production values challenging the long supremacy of French ACs in Bordeaux and the Loire Valley. Chile and South Africa aspire similarly. The wines are characterised by aromas of gooseberry, peapod, fresh-cut grass, even asparagus. Flavours are often described as 'grassy' or 'nettly'.

sec – Dry wine style. French.

secco – Dry wine style. Italian.

seco – Dry wine style. Spanish.

Semillon – White grape variety originally of Bordeaux, where it is blended with Sauvignon Blanc to make fresh dry whites and, when harvested very late in the season, the ambrosial sweet whites of Barsac, Sauternes and other appellations. Even in the driest wines, the grape can be recognised from its honeyed, sweet-pineapple, even banana-like aromas. Now widely planted in Australia and Latin America, and frequently blended with Chardonnay to make dry whites, some of them interesting.

sherry – The great aperitif wine of Spain, centred on the Andalusian city of Jerez (the name 'sherry' is an English mispronunciation). There is a lot of sherry-style wine in the world, but only the authentic wine from Jerez and the neighbouring producing centres of Puerta de Santa Maria and Sanlucar de Barrameda may label their wines as such. The Spanish drink real sherry – very dry and fresh, pale in colour and served well-chilled – called fino and manzanilla, and darker but naturally dry variations called amontillado, palo cortado and oloroso.

Shiraz – Australian name for the Syrah grape. The variety is the most widely planted of any in Australia, and makes red wines of wildly varying quality, characterised by dense colour, high alcohol, spicy fruit and generous, cushiony texture.

Somontano – Wine region of north-east Spain. Name means 'under the mountains' – in this case the Pyrenees – and the region has had DO status since 1984. Much innovative winemaking here, with New World styles emerging. Some very good buys. A region to watch.

souple – French wine-tasting term that translates into English as 'supple' or even 'docile' as in 'pliable', but I understand it in the vinous context to mean muscular but soft – a wine with tannin as well as soft fruit.

Spätlese – *See* QmP.

spirity – Some wines, mostly from the New World, are made from grapes so ripe at harvest that their high alcohol content can be detected through a mildly burning sensation on the tongue, similar to the effect of sipping a spirit. Young Port wines can be detectably spirity.

spritzy – Describes a wine with a gentle sparkle. Some young wines are intended to have this elusive fizziness; in others it is a fault.

spumante – Sparkling wine of Italy. Asti Spumante is the best known, from the town of Asti in the north-west Italian province of Piemonte. Many Prosecco wines are labelled as Spumante in style. The term describes wines that are fully sparkling. Frizzante wines have a less vigorous mousse.

stalky – A useful tasting term to describe red wines with flavours that make you think the stalks from the grape bunches must have been fermented along with the must (juice). Red Loire wines and youthful claret very often have this mild astringency. In moderation it's fine, but if it dominates it probably signifies the wine is at best immature and at worst badly made.

Stellenbosch – Town and region at the heart of South Africa's wine industry. It's an hour's drive from Cape Town and the source of much of the country's cheaper wine. Some serious-quality estate wines as well.

stony – Wine-tasting term for keenly dry white wines. It's meant to indicate a wine of purity and real quality, with just the right match of fruit and acidity.

structured – Good wines are not one-dimensional, they have layers of flavour and texture. A structured wine has phases of enjoyment: the 'attack', or first impression in the mouth; the middle palate as the wine is held in the mouth; and the lingering aftertaste.

sugar – *See* residual sugar.

sulphites – Nearly all wines, barring some esoteric 'natural' types of a kind not found in supermarkets are made with the aid of preparations containing sulphur to combat diseases in the vineyards and bacterial infections in the winery. It's difficult to make wine without sulphur. Even 'organic' wines need it. Because some people are sensitive to the traces of sulphur in some wines, worldwide health authorities insist wine labels bear the warning 'Contains sulphites'.

summer fruit – Wine-tasting term intended to convey a smell or taste of soft fruits such as strawberries and raspberries – without having to commit too specifically to which.

superiore – On labels of Italian wines, this is more than an idle boast. Under DOC(G) rules, wines must qualify for the *superiore* designation by reaching one or more specified quality levels, usually a higher alcohol content or an additional period of maturation. Frascati, for example, qualifies for DOC status at 11.5 per cent alcohol, but to be classified *superiore* must have 12 per cent alcohol.

sur lie – Literally, 'on the lees'. It's a term now widely used on the labels of Muscadet wines, signifying that after fermentation has died down, the new wine has been left in the tank over the winter on the lees – the detritus of yeasts and other interesting compounds left over from the turbid fermentation process. The idea is that additional interest is imparted into the flavour of the wine.

Syrah – The noble grape of the Rhône Valley, France. Makes very dark, dense wine characterised by peppery, tarry aromas. Now planted all over southern France and farther afield. In Australia it is known as Shiraz.

T

table wine – Wine that is unfortified and of an alcoholic strength, for UK tax purposes anyway, of no more than 15 per cent. I use the term to distinguish, for example, between the red table wines of the Douro Valley in Portugal and the region's better-known fortified wine, port.

Tafelwein – Table wine, German. The humblest quality designation, which doesn't usually bode very well.

tank method – Bulk-production process for sparkling wines. Base wine undergoes secondary fermentation in a large, sealed vat rather than in individual closed bottles. Also known as the Charmat method after the name of the inventor of the process. Prosecco is made by the tank method.

Tai – White grape variety of north-east Italy, a relative of Sauvignon Blanc. Also known in Italy as Tocai Friulano or, more correctly, Friulano.

Tannat – Black grape of south-west France, notably for wines of Madiran, and lately named as the variety most beneficial to health thanks to its outstanding antioxidant content.

tannin – Well known as the film-forming, teeth-coating component in tea, tannin is a natural compound that occurs in black grape skins and acts as a natural preservative in wine. Its noticeable presence in wine is regarded as a good thing. It gives young everyday reds their dryness, firmness of flavour and backbone. And it helps high-quality reds to retain their lively fruitiness for many years. A grand Bordeaux red when first made, for example, will have purply-sweet, rich fruit and mouth-puckering tannin, but after ten years or so this will have evolved into a delectably fruity, mature wine in which the formerly parching effects of the tannin have receded almost completely, leaving the shade of 'residual tannin' that marks out a great wine approaching maturity.

Tarrango – Black grape variety of Australia.

tarry – On the whole, winemakers don't like critics to say their wines evoke the redolence of road repairs, but I can't help using this term to describe the agreeable, sweet, 'burnt' flavour that is often found at the centre of the fruit in red wines from Argentina, Italy, Portugal and South Africa in particular.

TCA – Dreaded ailment in wine, usually blamed on faulty corks. It stands for 246 *trichloroanisol* and is characterised by a horrible musty smell and flavour in the affected wine. Thanks to technological advances made by cork manufacturers in Portugal – the leading cork nation – TCA is now in retreat.

tears – The colourless alcohol in the wine left clinging to the inside of the glass after the contents have been swirled. Persistent tears (also known as 'legs') indicate a wine of good concentration.

Tempranillo – The great black grape of Spain. Along with Garnacha (Grenache in France) it makes most red Rioja and Navarra wines and, under many pseudonyms, is an important or exclusive contributor to the wines of many other regions of Spain. It is also widely cultivated in South America.

Teroldego – Black grape variety of Trentino, northern Italy. Often known as Teroldego Rotaliano after the Rotaliano region where most of the vineyards lie. Deep-coloured, assertive, green-edged red wines.

terroir – French word for 'ground' or 'soil' has mystical meaning in vineyard country. Winemakers attribute the distinct characteristics of their products, not just to the soil conditions but to the lie of the land and the prevailing (micro)climate, all within the realm of terroir. The word now frequently appears on effusive back labels asserting the unique appeal of the wine. Some critics scoff that terroir is all imagined nonsense.

tinto – On Spanish labels indicates a deeply coloured red wine. Clarete denotes a paler colour. Also Portuguese.

Toro – Quality wine region east of Zamora, Spain.

Torrontes – White grape variety of Argentina. Makes soft, dry wines often with delicious grapey-spicy aroma, similar in style to the classic dry Muscat wines of Alsace, but at more accessible prices.

Touraine – Region encompassing a swathe of the Loire Valley, France. Non-AC wines may be labelled 'Sauvignon de Touraine'.

Touriga Nacional – The most valued black grape variety of the Douro Valley in Portugal, where port is made. The name Touriga now appears on an increasing number of table wines made as sidelines by the port producers. They can be very good, with the same spirity aroma and sleek flavours of port itself, minus the fortification.

Traminer – Grape variety, the same as Gewürztraminer.

Trebbiano – The workhorse white grape of Italy. A productive variety that is easy to cultivate, it seems to be included in just about every ordinary white wine of the entire nation – including Frascati, Orvieto and Soave. It is the same grape as France's Ugni Blanc. There are, however, distinct regional variations of the grape. Trebbiano di Lugana (also known as Turbiana) makes a distinctive white in the DOC of the name, sometimes very good, while Trebbiano di Toscana makes a major contribution to the distinctly less interesting dry whites of Chianti country.

Trincadeira Preta – Portuguese black grape variety native to the port-producing vineyards of the Douro Valley (where it goes under the name Tinta Amarella). In southern Portugal, it produces dark and sturdy table wines.

trocken – 'Dry' German wine. The description does have a particular meaning under German wine law, namely that there is only a low level of unfermented sugar lingering in the wine (9 grams per litre, if you need to know), and this can leave the wine tasting rather austere.

U

Ugni Blanc – The most widely cultivated white grape variety of France and the mainstay of many a cheap dry white wine. To date it has been better known as the provider of base wine for distilling into armagnac and cognac, but lately the name has been appearing on wine labels. Technology seems to be improving the performance of the grape. The curious name is pronounced 'OON-yee', and is the same variety as Italy's ubiquitous Trebbiano.

Utiel-Requena – Region and *Denominación de Origen* of Mediterranean Spain inland from Valencia. Principally red wines from Bobal, Garnacha and Tempranillo grapes grown at relatively high altitude, between 600 and 900 metres.

V

Vacqueyras – Village of the southern Rhône Valley of France in the region better known for its generic appellation, the Côtes du Rhône. Vacqueyras can date its winemaking history all the way back to 1414, but has only been producing under its own village AC since 1991. The wines, from Grenache and Syrah grapes, can be wonderfully silky and intense, spicy and long-lived.

Valdepeñas – An island of quality production amidst the ocean of mediocrity that is Spain's La Mancha region – where most of the grapes are grown for distilling into the head-banging brandies of Jerez. Valdepeñas reds are made from a grape they call the Cencibel – which turns out to be a very close relation of the Tempranillo grape that is the mainstay of the fine but expensive red wines of Rioja. Again, like Rioja, Valdepeñas wines are matured in oak casks to give them a vanilla-rich smoothness. Among bargain reds, Valdepeñas is a name to look out for.

Valpolicella – Red wine of Verona, Italy. Good examples have ripe, cherry fruit and a pleasingly dry finish. Unfortunately, there are many bad examples of Valpolicella. Shop with circumspection. Valpolicella Classico wines, from the best vineyards clustered around the town, are more reliable. Those additionally labelled *superiore* have higher alcohol and some bottle age.

vanilla – Ageing wines in oak barrels (or, less picturesquely, adding oak chips to wine in huge concrete vats) imparts a range of characteristics including a smell of vanilla from the ethyl vanilline naturally given off by oak.

varietal – A varietal wine is one named after the grape variety (one or more) from which it is made. Nearly all everyday wines worldwide are now labelled in this way. It is salutary to contemplate that until the present wine boom began in the 1980s, wines described thus were virtually unknown outside Germany and one or two quirky regions of France and Italy.

vegan-friendly – My informal way of noting that a wine is claimed to have been made not only with animal-product-free finings (*see* vegetarian wine) but without any animal-related products whatsoever, such as livestock manure in the vineyards.

vegetal – A tasting note definitely open to interpretation. It suggests a smell or flavour reminiscent less of fruit (apple, pineapple, strawberry and the like) than of something leafy or even root based. Some wines are evocative (to some tastes) of beetroot, cabbage or even unlikelier vegetable flavours – and these characteristics may add materially to the attraction of the wine.

vegetarian wine – Wines labelled 'suitable for vegetarians' have been made without the assistance of animal products for 'fining' – clarifying – before bottling. Gelatine, egg whites, isinglass from fish bladders and casein from milk are among the items shunned, usually in favour of bentonite, an absorbent clay first found at Benton in the US state of Montana.

Verdejo – White grape of the Rueda region in north-west Spain. It can make superbly perfumed crisp dry whites of truly distinctive character and has helped make Rueda one of the best white-wine sources of Europe. No relation to Verdelho.

Verdelho – Portuguese grape variety once mainly used for a medium-dry style of Madeira, also called Verdelho, but now rare. The vine is now prospering in Australia, where it can make well-balanced dry whites with fleeting richness and lemon-lime acidity.

Verdicchio – White grape variety of Italy best known in the DOC zone of Castelli di Jesi in the Adriatic wine region of the Marches. Dry white wines once known for little more than their naff amphora-style bottles but now gaining a reputation for interesting, herbaceous flavours of recognisable character.

Vermentino – White grape variety principally of Italy, especially Sardinia. Makes florally scented soft dry whites.

Vieilles vignes – Old vines. Many French producers like to claim on their labels that the wine within is from vines of notable antiquity. While it's true that vines don't produce useful grapes for the first few years after planting, it is uncertain whether vines of much greater age – say 25 years plus – than others actually make better fruit. There are no regulations governing the use of the term, so it's not a reliable indicator anyway.

Vin de France – In effect, the new Vin de Table of France's morphing wine laws. The label may state the vintage (if all the wine in the blend does come from a single year's harvest) and the grape varieties that constitute the wine. It may not state the region of France from which the wine originates.

vin de liqueur – Sweet style of white wine mostly from the Pyrenean region of south-westernmost France, made by adding a little spirit to the new wine before it has fermented out, halting the fermentation and retaining sugar.

vin de pays – 'Country wine' of France. Introduced in 1968 and regularly revised ever since, it's the wine-quality designation between basic Vin de France and AOC/AOP. Although being superseded by the more recently introduced IGP (*qv*), there are more than 150 producing areas permitted to use the description vin de pays. Some vin de pays areas are huge: the Vin de Pays d'Oc (referencing the Languedoc region) covers much of the Midi and Provence. Plenty of wines bearing this humble designation are of astoundingly high quality and certainly compete with New World counterparts for interest and value. *See* Indication Géographique Protégée.

vin de table – Formerly official designation of generic French wine, now used only informally. *See* Vin de France.

vin doux naturel – Sweet, mildly fortified wine of southern France. A little spirit is added during the winemaking process, halting the fermentation by killing the yeast before it has consumed all the sugars – hence the pronounced sweetness of the wine.

vin gris – Rosé wine from Provence.

Vinho de mesa – 'Table wine' of Portugal.

Vino da tavola – The humblest official classification of Italian wine. Much ordinary plonk bears this designation, but the bizarre quirks of Italy's wine laws dictate that some of that country's finest wines are also classed as mere vino da tavola (table wine). If an expensive Italian wine is labelled as such, it doesn't mean it will be a disappointment.

Vino de la Tierra – Generic classification for regional wines, Spain. Abbreviates to VdT.

Vino de mesa – 'Table wine' of Spain. Usually very ordinary.

vintage – The grape harvest. The year displayed on bottle labels is the year of the harvest. Wines bearing no date have been blended from the harvests of two or more years.

Viognier – A white grape variety once exclusive to the northern Rhône Valley in France where it makes expensive Condrieu. Now, Viognier is grown more widely, in North and South America as well as elsewhere in France, and occasionally produces soft, marrowy whites that echo the grand style of Condrieu itself. The Viognier is now commonly blended with Shiraz in red winemaking in Australia and South Africa. It does not dilute the colour and is confidently believed by highly experienced winemakers to enhance the quality. Steve Webber, in charge of winemaking at the revered De Bortoli estates in the Yarra Valley region of Victoria, Australia, puts between two and five per cent Viognier in with some of his Shiraz wines. 'I think it's the perfume,' he told me. 'It gives some femininity to the wine.'

Viura – White grape variety of Rioja, Spain. Also widely grown elsewhere in Spain under the name Macabeo. Wines have a blossomy aroma and are dry, but sometimes soft at the expense of acidity.

Vouvray – AC of the Loire Valley, France, known for still and sparkling dry white wines and sweet, still whites from late-harvested grapes. The wines, all from Chenin Blanc grapes, have a unique capacity for unctuous softness combined with lively freshness – an effect best portrayed in the demi-sec (slightly sweet) wines, which can be delicious and keenly priced.

Vranac – Black grape variety of the Balkans known for dense colour and tangy-bitter edge to the flavour. Best enjoyed in situ.

W

weight – In an ideal world the weight of a wine is determined by the ripeness of the grapes from which it has been made. In some cases the weight is determined merely by the quantity of sugar added during the production process. A good, genuine wine described as having weight is one in which there is plenty of alcohol and 'extract' – colour and flavour from the grapes. Wine enthusiasts judge weight by swirling the wine in the glass and then examining the 'legs' or 'tears' left clinging to the inside of the glass after the contents have subsided. Alcohol gives these runlets a dense, glycerine-like condition, and if they cling for a long time, the wine is deemed to have weight – a very good thing in all honestly made wines.

Winzergenossenschaft – One of the many very lengthy and peculiar words regularly found on labels of German wines. This means a winemaking co-operative. Many excellent German wines are made by these associations of growers.

woody – A subjective tasting note. A faintly rank odour or flavour suggesting the wine has spent too long in cask.

X

Xarel-lo – One of the main grape varieties for cava, the sparkling wine of Spain.

Xinomavro – Black grape variety of Greece. It retains its acidity even in the very hot conditions that prevail in many Greek vineyards, where harvests tend to over-ripen and make cooked-tasting wines. Modern winemaking techniques are capable of making well-balanced wines from Xinomavro.

Y

Yecla – Town and DO wine region of eastern Spain, close to Alicante, making interesting, strong-flavoured red and white wines, often at bargain prices.

yellow – White wines are not white at all, but various shades of yellow – or, more poetically, gold. Some white wines with opulent richness even have a flavour I cannot resist calling yellow – reminiscent of butter.

Z

Zibibbo – Sicilian white grape variety synonymous with north African variety Muscat of Alexandria. Scantily employed in sweet winemaking, and occasionally for drier styles.

Zierfandler – Esoteric white grape of Thermenregion, Austria. Aromatic dry wines and rare late-harvest sweet wines.

Zinfandel – Black grape variety of California. Makes brambly reds, some of which can age very gracefully, and 'blush' whites – actually pink, because a little of the skin colour is allowed to leach into the must. The vine is also planted in Australia and South America. The Primitivo of southern Italy is said to be a related variety, but makes a very different kind of wine.

Zweigelt – Black grape of Austria making juicy red wines for drinking young. Some wines are aged in oak to make interesting, heftier long-keepers.

Index